Young India's Most self-reflective read on Love. Dating. Marriage. Breakups. Expectations. Freedom. Pressure.

The
Paradox
Of
Modern

Love
and
Relationships

A Conscious Journey Through Doubts, Desires, And Decisions That Define Your Love Life.

DARSHAN

The Paradox of Modern Love and Relationships

Contents

Society has long conditioned us to believe that marriage is the ultimate sign of stability, the point at which life is considered "settled." We are constantly told, "Get married before it's too late." Deciding to get married is never a wrong decision but society rarely teaches us how to make the right choices. We are not taught how to find the right person, what actually matters in a marriage, how to navigate emotional complexity, or what marriage truly demands beyond the ceremony and rituals. No one tells us how to ask the right questions or evaluate compatibility, how to balance individuality with partnership, or how to face disagreements with maturity and empathy. And so, many people walk into marriage following societal scripts: unprepared, unaware, and often emotionally unequipped for the realities that come after the "big day."

INTRODUCTION

Marriage is celebrated across cultures as one of the most significant choices an individual can make a decision deeply influenced by love, tradition, societal expectations, and personal aspirations. For centuries, it has been regarded as a critical milestone, often perceived as a necessary step in life, sometimes even as a duty that one must fulfil. Yet, in our fast-evolving world, the traditional meanings and purposes of marriage are increasingly under scrutiny. They are being questioned, redefined, and in some instances, completely abandoned as people seek fulfilment in new and varied forms of relationships.

Why This Book Matters to You and Me

When we look around, we often see young people struggling with big decisions about love, relationships, and marriage. They face tough choices and sometimes end up making decisions they later regret. Sometimes they end up accepting the herd behaviour as an ultimate truth. In this fast-paced world, people often overlook the fundamental aspects of relationships and go by what they see around them. This book's prime goal is to ensure young generation has better understanding of culture, modern psychology, and ultimate truth in relationships, love, and marriages.

Throughout our schooling and education, we have never been taught about emotions, love, relationships, or marriage. We learn math, science, and history, yet the very foundation of human connection; how to navigate love, commitment, and emotional well-being remains largely untouched in formal education. Instead, society hands down narratives shaped by past experiences, cultural norms, and generational beliefs, many of which are biased, incomplete, or even detrimental to modern relationships.

What worked for one generation may no longer hold true in today's world, yet people continue to impose outdated ideals on relationships without considering the evolving complexities of love, personal aspirations, and individual growth.

Are love and passion enough? How do compatibility, personal growth, and emotional maturity play a role? What about career ambitions, family expectations, or the fear of loneliness? Can a fulfilling life be found outside of marriage? These are questions many hesitate to ask, yet they hold the key to making a decision that feels right, rather than one dictated by external forces.

This book aims to bridge that gap offering not just perspectives but also a deeper understanding of the emotional, psychological, and rational aspects of relationships. It is a conversation about love in its truest form, stripped of illusions, free from outdated conditioning, and rooted in the reality of what it means to love, commit, and evolve in today's world.

This book is designed not to hand you absolute answers or direct you down a predetermined path. Rather, its purpose is to serve as a guide in your journey of self-discovery. It will encourage you to question deeply held beliefs, to challenge societal norms, and to explore the many facets of romantic commitment. Through a thoughtful exploration of diverse perspectives and experiences, this book aims to help you uncover your own truths about love and commitment.

The journey through the paradox of love and marriage is complex and deeply personal. Each chapter of this book will delve into different aspects of marriage, from the joys and challenges of sharing your life with someone to the pressures and expectations that can come from outside and within. You'll read about the importance of personal growth, the realities of compatibility, and the courage it takes to pursue happiness, whether it's in union with another or in the affirmation of one's solitude.

Before you say 'yes' to a proposal, or decide to forge your own path alone, take a moment to pause and reflect. Consider this book as a companion in your journey—a tool to help you navigate the intricate realities of love and marriage.

The answers you seek are not prescribed here; instead, they lie within you, waiting to be discovered through introspection, understanding, and deliberate choice.

By engaging with the insights and stories shared in this book, you are taking an important step towards making a decision about marriage with clarity and conviction. Whether you choose to walk down the aisle or take a different path, this book will support you in making a choice that is authentically yours, one that contributes to your ongoing journey of personal fulfilment and happiness.

Parental guidance and societal teachings, while valuable, are often insufficient to navigate the modern paradox of love and relationships.

The Inspiration Behind This Book

The idea for this book came from watching/talking/observing friends and family I know as they tried to figure out their feelings and decisions about marriage. After a long interview, questions, psychological findings, I could observe that many of them making choices based on pressure, hurried feelings, or incomplete information. These choices often led to unhappiness and complications, not just for them but also for the people around them.

One of the best ways to learn is by looking at the experiences of others. This book brings together stories and lessons from different people's lives. By seeing what others have done right or wrong, we can learn important lessons for our own lives.

Your Journey to Self-Discovery

This book is also a journey into understanding yourself better. It invites you to think deeply about your values, hopes, and fears. It encourages you to ask questions, challenge common beliefs, and really think about what you want from life.

By the end of this book, the goal is for you to feel equipped and ready to make the best decisions for yourself, ones that lead to happiness and fulfilment in both love and life.

Author's Note on Sources and Stories

Except where external sources are explicitly cited in the references, the ideas, reflections, and narratives throughout this book are original works of the author, developed through observation, research, and personal insight.

Several chapters include real-life case studies or relationship stories. These are based on actual experiences, but names, locations, and identifying details have been changed to respect the privacy of individuals involved. In some instances, composite characters have been created to reflect common patterns or recurring themes in modern relationships.

This book does not offer prescriptive advice, but instead invites readers to reflect, question, and explore their own understanding through a conscious and honest lens.

Storyline is nothing but a unique story. I have numbered them to avoid confusion.

Before we move into chapters, here is a start of a story inspired by real life events.

The Paradox of Modern Love and Relationships

FROM FREE SPIRIT TO FIANCÉ: LIFE'S TURNING POINT

Storyline 1

Meet Ashish, my friend…the guy who could light up any room with his easy laughter and disarming charm. He had a way of making strangers feel like old friends and turning even the dullest evenings into memorable ones. Whether it was at college fests, office parties, or late-night chai breaks, Ashish was always the guy in the middle—laughing, teasing, breezing through life with the casualness of someone who believed the world would always be kind to him.

Commitment was a word he often avoided, not because he feared it, but because he never really saw the need for it. "Why complicate a good thing?" he'd joke when friends asked about his relationships. Love, to him, was fleeting and fun. Marriage? That was for later. Much later.

As Ashish approached his late twenties, the atmosphere in his household began to change. His mother, weary from health issues and the anxieties of life, started pressing the idea that Ashish should settle down. She believed that marriage could bring stability and happiness back into their home. Her insistence wasn't just a mere suggestion; it was almost a plea, a desperate hope that a new addition to the family might ease her burdens and bring a sense of order to their lives.

Ashish's father, having retired early, seemed to agree with this notion, albeit more quietly. In their middle-class household, every decision carried weight, and every change had a ripple effect. Ashish found himself torn between his easy-going nature and the weight of his parents' expectations. He wondered if perhaps they were right maybe a partner could bring the balance and happiness they so dearly missed.

For the first time in his life, Ashish started to entertain the idea of marriage seriously. It wasn't for love, not initially, nor was it for companionship as one might expect. Instead, it was a son's desire to fulfil his mother's wish, to bring a helping hand into the family that might lift some of the heaviness that had settled over their home. The concept of marriage as a stabilizing force began to take root in his mind, influenced by both the tangible needs of his family and the intangible hope for happier days.

Whenever I caught up with Ashish, he bombarded me with questions. "How should I go about this? What kind of girl should I look for?" His mind buzzed with the possibilities, and his usual light-heartedness was replaced by a serious tone, showing just how much this decision weighed on him. After sifting through two-three matrimonial profiles, Ashish's dilemma got resolved when he met a particular young woman. Something about her struck a different chord. Perhaps it was her demeanour or the way she spoke of her own family; whatever it was, Ashish decided she could be the one.

As we leave Ashish at this juncture, with a decision that feels more consequential than any he has ever made, his story pauses here. The outcomes of his choice—how it shapes his life and the fabric of his family will unfold in later chapters in portions.

CONTINUED IN LATER CHAPTERS....

Chapter 1

LOVE, COMPATIBILITY, AND THE ILLUSION OF "THE ONE"

Storyline 2 (Different from Storyline 1)

The air was crisp, and the café buzzed with quiet conversations. Aarav stirred his coffee absentmindedly, his mind clouded with questions. He had always believed in finding 'the one', that perfect person who would complete him, just as the movies and novels promised. Yet, here he was, struggling with doubts about his seemingly perfect relationship. Was love supposed to feel like this—filled with uncertainties, contradictions, and moments of disconnect?

Shraya sat across from him, her hands wrapped around a warm cup of tea. She had always imagined love to be effortless, something that, once found, would bring endless joy and fulfilment. Yet, as she looked at Aarav, she saw the same doubts reflected in his eyes. They had been together for three years, and while they cared deeply for each other, the cracks in their relationship widened when their decisions about few things started being different. Love, she realized, was not just about the magical connection they had felt in the beginning but about the choices they made every day.

For generations, love has been wrapped in layers of **myth and magic**, a notion that

somewhere out there exists a perfect match who completes us in every way.

Society, literature, and media have long endorsed the idea of a fated connection, one where a single moment or meeting transforms life entirely. Yet, upon closer look, this special image reveals itself as little more than a charming myth, an illusion that can distract us from understanding the true nature of human connection.

Our cultural narratives have often painted love as an effortless and inevitable bond, promoting the belief that destiny plays a significant role in our relationships. The expectation that there is one immaculate partner waiting to make all our problems vanish simplifies the multifaceted nature of love. In reality, relationships are not static or predestined; they are evolving processes that require constant care, negotiation, and growth. This oversimplification can lead to disillusionment when the messy, imperfect realities of life interfere with our idealized expectations.

In exploring the notion of destiny, we often refer to the uncontrollable forces that shape our lives elements that many label as luck, but which are, in essence, circumstances beyond our control.

This understanding prompts a fundamental question: should we resign ourselves entirely to fate and relinquish our agency? As Nawazuddin Siddiqui's dialogue (in Hindi) powerfully reminds us—

"भगवान भरोसे मत बैठिये क्या पता भगवान हमारे भरोसे बैठा हो,"

meaning "Don't just sit back and think God will do everything for you, who knows, maybe God is waiting for you to do something", there is an implicit call to action. This perspective challenges the idea of complete surrender to destiny, urging us instead to engage actively with life. While we must acknowledge that certain aspects of our journey are uncontrollable, it is equally important to recognize our power to influence outcomes through our decisions and efforts.

Raymond Knee, a well-known relationship researcher and psychologist introduced two major belief systems that people tend to adopt about relationships. He asked questions to people whether they believe in soulmate or not. What he found in the result is surprising. He found that there are some people who believe in soulmate and some who believed that relationship is a journey. Here are the explanations of them.

Destiny Beliefs (Soulmate Theory)

Individuals with strong destiny beliefs tend to think that there is one right person out there—a soulmate. They believe that compatibility is innate and fixed. If the relationship isn't perfect early on, they may assume it's not meant to last.

Growth Beliefs (Journey Theory)

The belief that successful relationships develop over time through effort, communication, and mutual adaptation. Individuals with growth beliefs understand that conflict is natural, and that love deepens as people work through challenges together.

Knee's research doesn't outright reject the concept of soulmates, but it does challenge the usefulness of the belief in soulmate thinking.

Believing in soulmates can be problematic when people expect perfect compatibility and give up quickly when issues arise. Couples who believe in growth and development tend to show more resilience, better conflict resolution, and long-term satisfaction.

In short:

"If you believe love is about finding the perfect one, you may give up too soon. But if you believe love is built, you are more likely to work through problems."

Love has always been a subject of deep conversation and countless attempts at understanding. But the truth is, no one can give love just one definition that fits everyone. It is not something that can be captured in a single idea or explanation. What love means to one person may be completely different from what it means to someone else. Instead of trying to find one definition of love, it is important to think about what love means to you. Love is an intense and unique feeling—it is something that can't always be put into words or fully understood. It is at once beautiful and mysterious, and it's something that everyone hopes to experience in their own way, even though it can be confusing or hard to grasp. The fact that love can seem so hard to define only makes it more powerful; it's a feeling that drives us all, even though we can't always explain why we're drawn to it or how it changes our lives.

At the heart of genuine connection lies compatibility, a concept far removed from the search for a flawless counterpart.

Compatibility is not about mirroring every quality or sharing identical interests; it is about finding balance amid differences, embracing the imperfections inherent in each of us, and nurturing a dynamic partnership where both individuals can flourish.

Real compatibility is rooted in mutual respect, open communication, and the willingness to evolve together. It calls for a deep understanding of one's own needs and values, as well as an appreciation for those of another, creating a foundation that supports both individual growth and collective harmony.

Moreover, the myth of "The One" often obscures the importance of self-discovery and personal development. When we anchor our happiness solely on finding an ideal partner, we may overlook the transformative journey of understanding ourselves. By shifting the focus inward, we recognize that the quality of our relationships is intricately tied to the quality of our own emotional well-being. True connection is built when individuals come together not as incomplete halves seeking to be made whole, but as whole beings who choose to share their lives and grow together, despite their imperfections.

In embracing this broader view of love, we are invited to let go of rigid expectations and instead cultivate relationships that reflect the complexities of real life. Love, in its truest form, is an ever-evolving dance—a blend of passion, compromise, and resilience. It challenges us to see beauty not in perfection, but in the unfolding journey of mutual support and shared growth. As we venture deeper into this exploration, the illusion of "The One" gradually gives way to a more authentic, nuanced understanding of connection—one that celebrates both individuality and togetherness in the face of life's uncertainties.

Is Compatibility Static?

Compatibility is much more than just having shared interests or similar backgrounds. It encompasses multiple layers of connection that contribute to a strong and lasting partnership. Emotional compatibility refers to how well partners handle conflicts, communicate during difficult moments, and provide mutual support. Intellectual compatibility involves the ability to engage in stimulating conversations, exchange ideas, and share similar values. Physical compatibility, on the other hand, speaks to the sexual and physical connection that fosters intimacy and brings partners closer. However, compatibility isn't a static trait—it evolves over time. As both partners grow and encounter new challenges, adjustments must be made to maintain the connection. This requires a continuous effort from both to adapt, communicate effectively, and nurture the relationship. In essence, true compatibility is built through mutual understanding, respect, and the proactive work both individuals put in to sustain the bond they share.

Ever Thought About The Kind of Partner You Really Want?

Even if you haven't written it down, your subconscious already knows what's acceptable to you and what isn't. That's why it's useful to create a list divided into two parts: a "must-have" list for those non-negotiable qualities, and a "should-have" list for traits that are nice to have but can be flexible. Remember, the idea of a perfect partner is just a dream—perfection is rare and unrealistic. By focusing on your essential requirements, you're more likely to find someone who truly complements you.

- **Must-Have List** – These are **non-negotiable values or traits** that you know you cannot compromise on (e.g., emotional stability, respect, shared life values).

- **Should-Have List** – These are **desirable traits** that would be nice to have but can be compromised to some extent (e.g., specific interests, physical attributes, financial status to a certain degree).

In our twenties, this list often leans toward surface-level traits like physical appearance, career success, and social status. At that stage, many qualities seem non-negotiable, driven by youthful ideals and societal expectations. However, as we grow older and our experiences accumulate, our priorities naturally shift. By the time we reach our thirties, the emphasis often moves away from superficial factors to deeper values such as emotional maturity, kindness, and effective problem-solving. Our past relationships, life's struggles, and growing self-awareness help refine our checklist, revealing what truly matters in a long-term partnership.

This evolution in our criteria is a reminder that chasing a perfect partner—a flawless match who ticks every box—is an unrealistic pursuit. Perfection is an illusion, and holding out for a 100% perfect match can lead to endless waiting and disappointment.

The paradox of love is that, when emotions come into play, our strict lists often take a backseat. You might meet someone who doesn't fulfil every criterion on paper, yet their ability to make you feel emotionally safe, seen, and understood may outweigh the absence of some surface-level traits. In such cases, the rigid boundaries of our checklist soften, and what remains is a profound connection based on shared values and mutual respect. Ultimately, the goal is to find a partner who aligns with your core values and with whom you can grow together recognizing that the ideal partner exists only in dreams, while real-world relationships thrive on understanding, adaptability, and the willingness to evolve together.

Sometimes, you may meet someone who makes you want to throw your entire list aside and surrender completely to the moment. It's a liberating, exhilarating experience that reminds you that the heart often knows best, even if it defies all the logical criteria you've set. This deep emotional connection is something to be embraced wholeheartedly. However, there's a subtle downside: in that moment of surrender, you might overlook or even forego some of your essential "must-have" values which can create a regret in long run. Yes, it's not easy.

External Factors

External pressures and social comparisons can significantly distort our perceptions of what makes a suitable partner. When we see friends with financially secure or exceptionally attractive partners, it's easy to fall into self-doubt and question our own choices. Thoughts like "Should I have aimed for someone more successful?" can creep in, undermining our confidence. Overcoming these comparisons requires a strong sense of self-awareness and a commitment to valuing our personal ideals over external validation.

In the realm of modern dating, the tendency to overthink and make snap judgments is all too common. Premature rejections or assumptions can arise when we analyse every behaviour before trust has the chance to develop naturally. A more positive approach is to give relationships time to unfold—observing and understanding each other without the pressure to decide too quickly. By holding back from instant judgments and allowing initial positivity to guide our interactions, we create space for genuine connections to emerge.

Ultimately, moving beyond the illusion of "The One" is about embracing the idea that a strong relationship is not simply found, but built. The notion of perfection can lead us to wait for an unattainable ideal, whereas true compatibility grows through mutual effort, understanding, and shared core values. Rather than chasing a flawless partner, the focus should be on fostering a relationship where both people can evolve together, building a foundation based on emotional alignment and the willingness to grow side by side.

As Aarav walked out of the café, he realized that love was not about finding the perfect person but about choosing someone and making the relationship work through shared effort and commitment. Love is not a passive fate; it is an active decision—a journey of understanding, compromise, and emotional maturity

"The happiest people are those who expect far less love than they give.
The unhappiest are those who constantly search for people to love them."

Chapter 2

THE INNER COMPASS: NAVIGATING RELATIONSHIP DILEMMAS WITH CLARITY AND COURAGE

Storyline 3

I met Kavya through mutual friends. She was an easy-going conversationalist but preferred calls over texts, which I found interesting. When I called her, she casually asked if we could meet for dinner. I agreed, not knowing that this conversation would soon lead into one of the most painful chapters of her life.

Over dinner, after exchanging a few pleasantries, I asked about her life before her new job and city. That's when she opened up about her horrible marriage.

"Things were fine at first," she said, "but suddenly, he started behaving differently. I assumed it was just a phase of marriage—something that couples go through. But then, I started noticing that even occasional romance was missing. It was like living with a stranger."

One day, she saw him at a shopping mall with a girl and another guy. Since they were three people together, she didn't want to overthink. But something inside her felt uneasy. That night, she subtly asked him about his day, bringing up the mall incident.

"I just wanted to see his reaction," she said. "And the moment I asked, he started feeling nervous."

That unease turned into suspicion, and she decided to check his phone. It was locked, but a notification popped up—a romantic message from someone else. The sight of it crushed her.

"I started feeling like I wasn't good enough. I lost confidence in myself. I withdrew, and slowly, we started fighting over the smallest things. At times, we didn't talk for months."

Months. I sat there, stunned. How can two people, married to each other, live under the same roof without speaking for months?

She recalled the breaking point.

"One day, I saw him with her again—this time around our house. That was it. I caught him. And finally, I gathered the courage to tell his parents."

She recounted this with an odd mix of relief and regret, as if the pain of silence had been worse than the betrayal itself.

The Lesson: Silence is Not Strength

Listening to Kavya, I realized how easily silence can become a slow poison in relationships. Many people believe they are choosing peace by avoiding confrontation, but in reality, they are delaying the inevitable and allowing pain to fester.

Kavya stayed in that house, in that relationship, for months without talking, hoping things would magically resolve or return to normal. But they never did. Instead, the lack of conversation only made things worse.

The lesson here is simple yet profound: **Do not stay silent.** If something feels wrong, talk about it. Confront the person, ask uncomfortable questions, and express what you feel. Silence does not resolve problems; it only prolongs suffering.

And if the truth is ugly, let it be. If a relationship is destined to turn negative, let it happen early rather than dragging it out for months or years.

Had Kavya confronted him earlier, she could have saved herself months of self-doubt, anxiety, and loneliness. Had she prioritized conversation over ego, she might have found either resolution or closure much sooner.

Marriage—or any relationship—cannot survive without communication. It is not just about love, companionship, or shared responsibilities. It is about dialogue, about facing reality together. If there is no conversation, there is no solution.

And if a relationship ever reaches a point where silence feels safer than speaking, perhaps it's time to question whether that relationship is worth staying in.

Speak Your Truth or Maintain Peace?

This is one of the most paralyzing inner dilemmas. You know the truth will shake things up—perhaps cause a storm. But silence eats away at your authenticity. So, you smile while your soul whispers for freedom.

Peace that comes from silence and suppression is not real peace—it's a temporary truce. Eventually, the unspoken truth finds other ways to express itself—through passive-aggression, emotional withdrawal, or breakdown.

Speaking your truth doesn't guarantee that others will accept it. But it ensures that you don't abandon yourself.

The question to ask: Is this relationship sacred enough to hold my truth?

Conversation is the Lifeline of Any Marriage or Relationship

In any relationship—whether dating, marriage, or long-term companionship—conversation is the foundation upon which everything else is built. You can travel to exotic places, enjoy lavish parties, have incredible physical intimacy, and experience moments of joy, but at the end of the day, what truly sustains a relationship is genuine companionship, and that comes from deep, meaningful conversations.

A fulfilling relationship isn't just about sharing experiences—it's about sharing thoughts, emotions, and perspectives. The ability to communicate openly, honestly, and respectfully determines the strength of the bond between two people. When partners can talk about their fears, dreams, past life, vulnerabilities, and everyday experiences without judgment, that's when true intimacy is formed—one that goes beyond the superficial layers of physical attraction or external excitement.

Respect in conversation is key. It's not just about talking but also about listening, understanding, and making space for each other's voice. Many relationships fail not because of a lack of love, but because of a lack of communication. When conversation dies, so does the emotional connection.

At its core, a life partner is someone you want to talk to every day, for the rest of your life. That is what keeps a relationship alive—not just passion, not just shared responsibilities, but the comfort of knowing that there's someone with whom you can share your thoughts, laugh at your deepest fears, and find solace in their words when everything else feels uncertain.

The Unsung Power of Humour in Relationships

Humour is one of the most underrated but powerful forces in a relationship. In a world full of pressures, seriousness, and emotional heaviness, having someone to laugh with is not just a luxury—it's a necessity. You can't romance all the time. You can't have sex all the time. You can't engage in deep, serious talks all the time. But you can laugh often, and that's what keeps the bond fresh, joyful, and alive. Pulling each other's legs, engaging in playful competition, and sharing private jokes adds flavour to the routine and lightness to the baggage we all carry. Humour breaks tension, heals small emotional wounds, and reminds couples that love doesn't always have to be profound—it can be silly, spontaneous, and wonderfully ordinary. A couple that can laugh together, especially in tough times, often finds their way back to each other faster. Because at the end of the day, life is more amazing when it's treated like a movie full of laughter, mischief, and light moments.

Isn't It Risky? What if It Doesn't Work Out?

Many people hold back from investing time and energy into relationships because of the fear of failure or past disappointments. They think, *"What if it goes wrong again?"* and, as a result, they hesitate to open up, commit, or give their full effort. While this fear is understandable, it also creates a self-fulfilling cycle of emotional stagnation—one where relationships never reach their full potential because one or both partners refuse to truly invest in them.

Just like in investing, you cannot generate returns without making an investment. Love, trust, and emotional security do not grow on their own; they require time, patience, and a willingness to take calculated risks. Of course, this doesn't mean investing blindly—it requires scrutiny, self-awareness, and choosing wisely. But if one constantly holds back due to fear, they will never experience the depth and fulfilment that relationships can offer.

In both life and relationships, growth comes from engagement, not avoidance. Choosing to invest emotionally, intellectually, and spiritually is what leads to true connection and personal transformation. The key is to balance caution with courage, ensuring that while you protect yourself from unnecessary pain, you do not block yourself from genuine happiness and fulfilment.

"Half the work in finding love is simply believing that the kind of love you seek actually exists."

Does It Work Always?

It's like expecting a 100% guaranteed outcome from a business venture—sounds ideal, but that's not how real value is created. Businesses fail. Relationships fail. But people still try. Why? Because great outcomes demand risk.

If you're aiming for extraordinary love, you can't take only safe routes. Seeking clarity by trial isn't mediocrity—it's part of the process. Just like in entrepreneurship, not every attempt is meant to succeed. Some are meant to teach, some to transform.

Running away from emotional failure might protect you—but it also limits you. You may end up in a safe, predictable relationship, just like someone sticking to a steady job. Nothing wrong with it. But don't confuse safety with greatness.

True love, like any meaningful venture, comes with uncertainty. And the ones who dare to explore—knowing it might break them—are often the ones who end up finding something truly rare.

Apologies and Relationships

In any relationship, one of the most essential acts of emotional maturity is the willingness to acknowledge when you're wrong. Yet, most people find themselves caught in the habit of defending, deflecting, or retaliating, rather than simply owning their mistake. They become skilled at identifying red flags in the other person yet rarely pause to introspect on their own flaws or missteps—even when they are clearly aware of them. This lack of self-reflection creates a toxic loop of blame and ego, where conversations become battles, not bridges.

One of the biggest roadblocks to a healthy relationship is being non-apologetic. People often withhold apologies not because they didn't make a mistake, but because they feel their partner had wronged them earlier—and this becomes their form of emotional scorekeeping. But that's not how emotional growth works. Every situation should be treated on its own merit. An apology should not be a transaction—it should be a reflection of empathy, ownership, and care.

Successful marriages are built on deep friendship, mutual respect, and effective conflict resolution.

Non-apologetic behaviour often stems from emotional detachment, unchecked ego, or a deep-seated need to always be right. But in love, being right matters less than being real. A sincere apology has the power to heal wounds, restore trust, and reaffirm emotional safety. Without it, resentment festers, and the distance grows—not just between two people, but between who we are and who we're capable of becoming in a relationship.

Biggest Enemy of Relationships

One of the biggest enemies of relationships today is not conflict or distance—it's boredom and emotional saturation. In the age of instant gratification and emotional oversupply, love, care, and attention are often given in excess early on, leaving little space for longing, mystery, or natural growth. While it's human nature to feel overwhelmed by "too much," what people often fail to recognize is that in real, meaningful relationships, the absence of a person—even for a day—creates a void that says more than their presence ever could. But when a relationship ends because of emotional burnout or perceived suffocation, people carry that memory forward. In their next bond, they start holding back, becoming emotionally guarded, afraid of repeating the same pattern. This leads to a universal, self-sabotaging cycle—where one partner gives too much too soon, and the other, in future relationships, gives too little out of fear. This emotional overcorrection weakens the foundation of genuine connection, making it harder for love to thrive naturally and sustainably.

Respect is the New Love

"At the heart of every healthy relationship is not just love, but respect—the quiet, steady force that holds everything together when emotions waver. Respect means valuing your partner not just for who they are today, but for who they're trying to become. It means admiring their abilities, recognizing their skills, appreciating their efforts, and never diminishing their worth based on income, habits, or differences in worldview. Real respect doesn't disappear when flaws appear—it deepens. Because in marriage or long-term love, you don't discover all imperfections upfront. They surface slowly, layer by layer, like truths revealing themselves over time. And when they do, respect is what stops you from judging. It helps you hold space for growth instead of rushing to criticize. You see the gaps, but you choose to stand beside them, not above them. You may not agree with all of their beliefs or habits, but you choose to understand instead of control. That's the kind of respect that doesn't just keep love alive—it strengthens it. When two people feel respected in a relationship, they don't shrink to fit each other—they rise, evolve, and expand together."

Opposite Gender Friendship While in a Relationship

This question has always intrigued me because it doesn't have a black-and-white answer. I do believe it's possible to have meaningful, platonic friendships with the opposite gender, even while being in a relationship. But I've also come to realize that how it's handled matters more than the relationship itself.

If I'm in a relationship, I know how important it is to maintain transparency. It's not about permission, it's about comfort. I wouldn't want my partner to feel like I'm hiding something or giving more emotional space to someone else. Friendships should feel light, respectful, and naturally aligned with the relationship I value.

If someone becomes a source of emotional closeness beyond what I share with my partner, that's when I know the line is blurred. Trust is built through openness, not secrecy. And if I ever feel the need to hide a friendship, that's a sign I'm not being fully honest with myself or with the person I'm with.

Jealousy arises not always from insecurity but from secrecy or imbalance in transparency. Opposite-gender friendships are possible, but only when both partners feel emotionally safe, and boundaries are understood and respected.

Friendships don't need to end, but prioritization and openness matter. If a friendship feels threatening to your partner, don't dismiss their concern discuss and align boundaries together.

Fight for It or Surrender Gracefully?

Not every relationship is meant to be fought for, and not every ending is a failure. The wisdom lies in knowing the difference.

Fighting for love means:

- You're both willing to grow, communicate, and evolve.

- There is mutual respect, even during chaos.

- There's a shared willingness to understand, not just to be right.

But when the fight becomes one-sided, when your emotional effort is constant, or when hope becomes your only glue—it might be time to surrender.

Surrender is not weakness. It is the highest form of acceptance. It means you're choosing truth over illusion, growth over stagnation, and self-preservation over sacrifice.

Walking Away as an Act of Love

Sometimes, love asks you to stay and fight. Other times, it asks you to let go with grace.

The idea that leaving someone means failure is deeply flawed. Walking away can often be the kindest thing you do—for both of you.

Staying in a relationship where growth has stopped, where resentment is louder than affection, or where you are constantly shrinking to fit, is not love. It is fear in disguise.

Walking away can mean:

- I love myself enough to no longer stay where I am not valued.
- My self-love is louder now than my fear of being alone.
- I care for you enough to set us both free from something that's no longer blooming.
- Healing may be hard, but it's more honest than pretending this works.

"When we meet someone who ticks a few important boxes, perhaps they're kind, attractive, ambitious, or share similar life goals-we often find ourselves going out of the way to win their affection. We begin adjusting to their preferences, aligning with their routines, and sometimes even moulding parts of our personality to match what we think they're looking for. Since we've been the one to initiate or express interest, the power dynamic subtly shifts, and the other person now begins to evaluate us against their internal criteria. In our eagerness to be chosen, we often treat this process like an achievement believing that if we meet all their expectations, we will naturally progress into something long-term, even marriage. But in the midst of this effort, we often overlook key elements like balanced emotional compatibility, aligned thought processes, shared values, or basic common sense. We overlook 'Self'."

Chapter 3

EXPECTATIONS, AND COMPARISONS: FAMILY & SOCIETY

Storyline 1 Continued....

After Ashish got engaged, it felt like a wave of relief swept through his household. His mother—who had long been weighed down by health issues and unspoken worries—seemed lighter, more at ease. She smiled more often, her energy returned slowly, and even her health showed signs of improvement. It was as if Ashish had lifted a heavy emotional burden from her shoulders.

The home that once echoed with quiet concern began to fill with laughter again. Conversations were livelier, the air lighter. And somewhere amidst the chaos of wedding preparations, we saw glimpses of the old Ashish—the cheerful, joking, carefree version of him.

Since the girl's family was in a hurry to marry off their younger daughter quickly—given that her older brother was already planning his own wedding—Ashish decided to get married within two months of the engagement. The ceremony was intimate but full of joy. A small event yet filled with heart.

Ashish looked happy, but his mother looked the happiest.

After the wedding, Ashish became distant. Not emotionally cold, but simply unavailable. We didn't see him around much anymore. Our usual hangouts faded into occasional phone calls, and even those were hurried.

One day, I insisted that we catch up over dinner. He agreed and surprised me by bringing his wife, Aarti, along.

They arrived, and while everything looked fine on the surface, it didn't take long to sense some tension. It came up casually—over a small disagreement about planning a weekend trip.

I asked gently, "Is everything alright? Can I help?"

Ashish paused, hesitated. Then, with a tired sigh, he began to share.

"Aarti loves traveling and fashion," he said, looking at her briefly. "And somehow... that's become a point of conflict at home. There's always a fight."

Before he could finish, Aarti, clearly holding back frustration, jumped in:

"Let me tell you what actually happens. I don't overspend. I don't ask for money from anyone. I work. I earn. But somehow, my mother-in-law always makes me feel like I spend too much or that I don't save enough. She doesn't like us going on trips.

I can't do all the household work—because I work full-time, and I love my job. But she expects more. Sometimes, she even says, *'What's the point of having a daughter-in-law if she can't help with the house?'* It's exhausting. I've told Ashish many times, but he hasn't tried to speak with her."

Ashish's voice broke slightly as he replied:

"What do I even say? My mother has a chronic condition. She's fragile."

Aarti looked at him, trying to stay composed, but the pain slipped through her words.

"Then let's hire a maid. That's what I've suggested."

Ashish nodded slowly. "Yes, we can... but my father refuses to eat food made by anyone except my mother."

Aarti scoffed, with a faint, bitter smile.

"*Fir toh baat hi khatam hai.* (Hindi) Why are we even talking about this?"

The silence that followed said more than any words could. I sat there quietly, listening. I didn't feel like offering advice at that moment. It didn't feel right—not with both of them sitting there, still raw from the unspoken hurts and lingering exhaustion.

I knew I had to talk to Ashish alone.

His story, like many others, had shifted from a son fulfilling a wish to a man stuck between loyalty, love, and growing resentment. What started as a joyful act of balance had turned into a balancing act—with no clear ground beneath his feet.

This is where we pause Ashish's journey once more. But his story, like most marriages, is just getting started. It will return in future chapters—reshaped by conflict, love, silence, and decisions that none of us saw coming.

Family is our first social network—a mosaic of traditions, shared histories, and unspoken rules that shape our sense of self from the earliest days. In the gentle embrace of family, we find warmth and security; yet as we grow, this same structure often reveals its intricate web of expectations. These early lessons in loyalty and belonging come with a dual message: cherish the roots that ground you but also be mindful of the branches that reach out toward your own destiny.

The Familial Bonds

In every relationship and life choice, the impact of our family is undeniable. From childhood, our perceptions of love and commitment are filtered through the lens of familial interactions. The approval we seek from parents, siblings, and elders can feel like both a blessing and a burden. In many cases, the echoes of their hopes and dreams create a powerful backdrop against which we measure our decisions. This familial influence is not inherently negative; it provides a foundation of support and continuity, but it can also impose invisible limits on the paths we dare to take.

As one matures, the desire to honour family traditions can evolve into a compelling force that sometimes stifles personal ambition. The pursuit of acceptance—rooted in cultural customs and generational expectations—may conflict with the intrinsic need for self-expression and individual fulfilment. Many find themselves caught in the delicate balance between satisfying family expectations and nurturing their own inner voice. The struggle to maintain this equilibrium is often an unspoken battle, where every decision carries the weight of past legacies and future hopes. In the name of family, finding a wealthy and stable family leads to failure in right choices.

Old Matrimonial thing

In the tapestry of Indian matrimonial traditions, the contrast between past and present is striking. In olden times, marriages were arranged without the couple even meeting—decisions were made by parents and grandparents who weighed families, reputations, casts, and long-held traditions. There was no opportunity for a conversation or a shared glance; the union was a matter of duty and legacy. Today, while the essence of arranged marriage endures, the process has evolved dramatically. Potential partners now have multiple meetings, a chance to truly connect and "taste the fruit before buying." Yet, this shift is not uniform across the country. In semi-urban and rural areas, the age-old influence of family remains strong, especially when young individuals are still finding their footing. In contrast, metro cities are witnessing a gradual decline in familial control as education, exposure, and personal experiences empower the youth to make choices that resonate with their own hearts.

Parent's role in decision making

Parents often face social pressure from relatives and friends, especially during family gatherings. When questions about their child's marriage begin to surface, the pressure can intensify. Remarks like, "Why isn't she/he married yet?" or examples from others about how delaying marriage can cause problems, only add to their concerns. These comments can make parents feel inadequate or as if they're falling behind in fulfilling societal expectations. The constant comparison and judgment around marriage timing can lead parents to push their children toward making rushed decisions, neglecting their child's readiness and emotional well-being in the process. This pressure underscores the importance of allowing individuals to make personal decisions based on their own readiness, rather than being swayed by the opinions of others.

In metro cities, people have more freedom to choose their own partners, but family approval still plays a role. Many parents focus on material things like income, a good house, a car, and a strong social status. They often stress the importance of a stable income and assets, sometimes overlooking whether the couple truly connects emotionally. Phrases like

"We just want the best for you"

may seem caring, but they can hide deeper expectations and put subtle pressure on the decision-making process.

Parents often believe they know best about how the world works and what society is like. While their experience gives them a strong perspective, their views are based on how relationships worked in the past, not necessarily how they work today. Their experiences, shaped by hardships and high ambitions, can sometimes lead to biases. For example, parents who struggled while aiming high may favour families with wealth and stability. This belief, though understandable, might not always match the reality of modern relationships.

As the family builds the culture of checking the materialistic checklists, the youngsters will also try to find partner which can fit into filters of parents.

Family expectations often lean heavily on material success—good jobs, a nice house, and a fancy car—which can overshadow the importance of emotional connection. Even when all these surface markers are met, a marriage can struggle if the deep bond between partners is missing. This focus on material stability shapes young minds from an early age. Children grow up internalizing these checklists, learning to value wealth and status, sometimes at the expense of finding someone who truly connects with them on an emotional level. As these young individuals mature, many start to see that genuine love cannot be measured by assets alone.

"You marry into a family, not just a person."

This statement is overvalued. While it may be true in some respects, the partner is still the most important factor. And when you assess the family, it's not just about their wealth, stability, and their social recognition. It's about how supportive the family can be.

o   Many individuals, consciously or unconsciously, prioritize family acceptance over their own emotional compatibility with their partner.

o   The problem is families often judge a marriage's "suitability" through materialistic checklists—financial stability, social status, etc.—rather than relationship depth.

o   This creates pressure to marry into a "good family" rather than ensuring the chosen partner is truly the right fit.

One common mistake is when male's parents see marriage as a way to find a female who will handle all the household work.

Marriage should be about companionship, emotional support, and sharing life together, not about hiring someone to manage a home. When families assume that one partner must take care of everything at home, they miss the chance to build a true partnership.

It's Not the Checklist Task

Some parents see marriage as just a task to be completed—a transaction that marks the end of their duty. They feel a sense of relief once the wedding is over, forgetting that their role should not end there.

Many parents often see marriage as a milestone that should be reached by a certain age, but their true role should be to ensure that their child is ready—emotionally, mentally, physically, and financially—before taking that step.

Instead of pushing for marriage as a check-off box, they might ask simple questions like, "Are you ready for marriage?" or "Do you feel prepared to share your life with someone?" It's important for them to consider whether issues like career, finances, or personal growth might be holding their child back, and to offer support if needed. Marriage should happen when a person is fully prepared, not just because society expects it. Likewise, parents should respect their child's choice, even if it means delaying marriage or choosing not to marry at all. A delay doesn't mean a rejection of marriage forever; it often means the child is taking time to be fully ready, and that is perfectly okay. By focusing on readiness and respecting individual choices, parents can help create a healthier, more supportive path toward lasting relationships.

Parent's role should be to:

- **Ask meaningful questions:** *"Are you ready for marriage?" "Do you need more time?"*

- **Support their child's emotional needs** and not force marriage based on age or societal timelines.

- **Respect their child's choice**—whether they want to delay marriage, choose a non-traditional partner, or not marry at all.

Values and Traditions

Many parents hold a strong set of traditional values that they expect their children to follow, including the choice of a life partner. They believe that these values are the key to a stable and successful life. However, when these expectations are pushed too hard, children can feel overwhelmed

However, a real clash emerges when modern, independent perspectives meet traditional values. In metro cities, where people are more exposed to new ideas, young minds often lean towards making decisions based on personal fulfilment rather than just ticking off material boxes. Yet, their families, influenced by long-standing beliefs and past hardships, may still prioritize stability and social status. This generational gap creates tension, as many youngsters hesitate to introduce their partners to their families, worried about cultural or lifestyle clashes. In this mix of materialistic checklists and evolving personal values, the true challenge lies in balancing the weight of tradition with the pursuit of authentic emotional connection.

Young individuals struggle with the dual identity of who they are at home vs. who they've become in the outside world. The cultural shift due to moving to metro cities leads to delayed marriages, as individuals take time to reconcile their values with family expectations.

Happens frequently when youngsters went out to bigger cities from small town and adopt the culture leaving a wide difference between their thought process, education, way of life and that of family. Some choose partners from similar backgrounds (e.g., those who also moved from small towns to big cities) to ensure that their partner understands their dilemma and is better equipped to balance both worlds.

Some people slowly condition their families by gently introducing new ideas during casual conversations, sharing reallife examples of happy marriages that defy traditional norms. Others choose partners from similar cultural backgrounds, making it easier to balance modern values with longheld family expectations. There are also those who set clear boundaries, firmly stating, "This is the person I choose," and hoping that their family will eventually put their child's happiness first.

In some cases, individuals even delay marriage—or choose lifelong singlehood—to avoid sacrificing their own fulfilment for the sake of family acceptance. These varied approaches highlight how difficult it can be to bridge the gap between evolving personal perspectives and the persistent financial and social checklists that families often hold dear.

Expectations and Contributions in Relationships

One common thread that often entangles the fabric of relationships is the weight of expectations. Many people enter into a relationship with a checklist of qualities and virtues they hope to find in their partner, believing that fulfilling these criteria will inevitably lead to love. It's a comforting notion, to think that love will blossom fully formed once our expectations are met. However, this mindset overlooks a fundamental aspect of successful relationships: mutual contribution and fulfilment.

Expectations, in themselves, are not inherently negative. They can guide us towards what we desire in a partner and help us define our boundaries and deal breakers. The problem arises when these expectations become rigid benchmarks that overshadow the genuine qualities of the person in front of us. If the sole basis for love is how well someone conforms to a preconceived list of traits, one might miss out on a deeper, more meaningful connection that could flourish from appreciating their genuine self.

Furthermore, it is essential to reflect on what one brings to the table. Relationships are not merely about finding someone who checks all the boxes; they are about two individuals contributing to a shared life. If one enters a relationship with high demands but offers little in return, the imbalance can lead to dissatisfaction and resentment. It's akin to wanting a gourmet meal at a potluck but only bringing a bag of chips. True partnership requires both parties to contribute equally and valuably.

Before setting standards for others, it's beneficial to conduct a self-assessment. What are your strengths? What unique qualities do you bring to a relationship? How do you plan to contribute to the mutual growth and happiness of the partnership?

Answering these questions can provide a clearer perspective on what you seek and what you are prepared to give in return. This balanced approach not only fosters a healthier relationship but also attracts someone who values and resonates with the qualities you offer.

If expectations are non-negotiable, and you find yourself unwilling to adjust them, then patience becomes crucial. Holding out for the "right" one—who not only meets your expectations but whom you can meet theirs equally—might mean a longer wait, but it can also lead to a more fulfilling relationship. It's important to recognize, however, that even the "right" one will have imperfections, and learning to appreciate these imperfections is part of growing together in a realistic and loving partnership.

Social Comparisons

In today's world, choosing a life partner is never just a personal decision—it is influenced by the many voices and comparisons around us. We often hear thoughts like,

"My friend's partner earns so much more—should I aim for someone financially stronger?"

"My cousin married someone who fits perfectly into their family—should I be worried my partner isn't as socially compatible?"

"Everyone in my circle is with someone highly successful or attractive—am I settling by not prioritizing that?"

which can make us question our own choices. Social pressure and constant comparisons can lead us to doubt what we truly value, making us feel that we are missing out or settling for less.

This constant measuring against others can create feelings of jealousy and dissatisfaction, as we start focusing on what we think our relationship lacks rather than on its real strengths. The pressure to match external benchmarks can pull us away from our true desires and the unique connection we share with our partner.

Jealousy builds up, not because your partner lacks something important to you, but because social benchmarks make you feel like you're missing out.

To overcome this, it is important to reconnect with our core values, appreciate the emotional security and fulfilment our relationship offers, and remember that every relationship comes with its own set of challenges. Ultimately, letting go of these external pressures and trusting our own journey can help us build a relationship that is genuine and deeply satisfying.

- Look within and reconnect with your core values.
- Ask yourself: "Is this something I genuinely value, or is this influenced by what others have?"
- Reflect on: "Does my partner make me feel fulfilled and secure, regardless of what others think?"
- Acknowledge feelings of comparison but don't let them dictate decisions.
- Practice gratitude for what your relationship brings. Focus on the emotional security, compatibility, and happiness that your relationship offers, rather than superficial comparisons.
- Recognize that every relationship has trade-offs. The "perfect" relationship you see externally may have its own set of challenges.

Negotiating the Space Between Tradition and Self

In the modern landscape, the challenge is not to reject the values that have shaped us, but to reinterpret them in a way that aligns with personal truths. This journey of negotiation is deeply personal and ever evolving. It involves redefining what family means in a world where individual aspirations often diverge from collective ideals. The path forward requires introspection, open dialogue, and the courage to set boundaries that honour both tradition and the pursuit of personal authenticity. In this space, compromise does not signify surrender but rather an opportunity to create a new narrative—one where respect for the past meets the promise of a self-determined future.

Embracing a Balanced Perspective

Ultimately, the interplay between family expectations and personal desires is a dynamic process. It invites us to explore the origins of our beliefs and to question whether the weight of tradition should dictate our future choices. The journey toward a balanced perspective involves acknowledging the valuable support that family provides while also recognizing the need for personal growth and self-reliance. This chapter is an invitation to reflect on how our relationships with family shape our decisions, and to consider how we might navigate these influences with both gratitude and discernment. In doing so, we pave the way for a more conscious and authentic life—one that honours both the legacy of our past and the promise of our individual potential.

"The person who understand life well and have good common sense will handle relationships well and likely to have clarity in relationship. Not necessary that intelligent or having thoughts of clarity in people will have successful marriages. And there is no correlation. Just that clarity of thoughts will lead to clarity in relationship and marriage."

"

Can a Man Who's Still Struggling Financially Be Taken Seriously in Dating?

As someone who has seen the ups and downs of early career phases, I've felt the pressure of not being "financially ready" for love. Society often ties a man's worth to his earnings. I've seen how that creates a silent weight, the fear of not being chosen because I'm still building.

But I also know that money alone doesn't make someone a good partner. I value consistency, intent, and emotional maturity. And I believe a man who's willing to grow, learn, and support emotionally can offer something far more valuable than a loaded bank account. At the same time, I won't deny that financial stability matters, not for luxury, but for peace, planning, and shared responsibility.

Don't dismiss a man who's still figuring it out, especially if his direction is clear and his character is strong.

Don't let money define your worth, let your growth do that.

Chapter 4

THE CURRENCY OF COMMITMENT: FINANCIAL FABRIC OF MARRIAGE

Storyline 1 Continued....

That night, after the tense dinner, I called Ashish. "Ashish," I said, "I really think you need to break the ice. Just sit with both of them—your mom and Aarti. Try to talk things through calmly. Especially when they're both in the room, maybe you can step in and explain things, so it doesn't turn into a blame game. Can you try that?"

Ashish sighed heavily on the other end of the line.

"Leave it, yaar. I don't want to get into all this. We'll figure it out. Let's not talk about it."

I didn't push him. He wasn't ready.

A Few Days Later...

Ashish called me one morning. "Can we meet?" he asked, his voice unusually low.

We met at a quiet café. He looked drained—physically there, but mentally somewhere else.

"We had a big fight this morning," he said, avoiding eye contact. "Aarti left. She's gone to her parents' house. She said she doesn't want to stay anymore."

I sat in silence for a moment, then asked gently, "What happened?"

He took a deep breath and began explaining. It was the same old pattern—little arguments snowballing into big fights. But this time, the trigger had been a new iPhone.

"Aarti bought it recently," he said. "She paid for it herself, from her salary, but somehow it became a thing at home. Mom thought it was wasteful, Dad stayed quiet, and I... I didn't say anything again."

I looked at him and shook my head. "Ashish... remember what I said that night? You needed to talk—to both sides. But you brushed it off."

He nodded; guilt written all over his face. "I know. I should've. I just... didn't want to stir things up more."

"Well, now what?" I asked.

"I'll talk to Aarti," he said, trying to sound hopeful.

"That's good," I replied. "But that's not enough anymore. You have to talk to your parents too. This isn't about choosing sides—it's about creating understanding. Everyone needs to know what's expected when it comes to finances, lifestyle, and housework. Let each person speak. Then come to some kind of mutual ground. Otherwise, this won't stop."

He paused for a long moment, then nodded slowly. "Yeah. I can do that."

We didn't say much after that. The moment was heavy filled with unspoken truths and the quiet realization that growing up sometimes means having conversations you don't want to have.

And once again, Ashish's story pauses—not with resolution, but with the first signs of responsibility.

Financials Before Marriage

Marriage is often seen as an emotional union, but its economic and financial dimensions play a crucial role in shaping relationships. In many societies, marriage is not just about love and companionship but also about financial stability, social status, and resource sharing.

In many cultures, including India, financial stability is a significant factor when families consider potential matches, especially in arranged marriages. Often, the male partner is expected to be the primary provider, which leads families to place considerable focus on his income, job, and social standing.

Family values that stress financial stability, property, and social status can create a cycle where even young people start to prioritize these factors when choosing a partner. This often leads to a kind of "filter-based matchmaking," where the search for a life partner is driven more by material markers than by emotional connection or shared values. Even in love marriages, there's often an unspoken check—questions like,

"Will my parents approve of their job, house, and income?"

—that guide decisions before the couple even gets to know each other deeply. This implicit screening means that deep emotional compatibility can sometimes take a backseat to material concerns, reinforcing traditional expectations and making it harder for individuals to follow their heart completely.

The family's criteria are often surface level, but relationships are built on deeper foundations.

However, the common misconception lies in equating financial stability solely with monthly income. For example, a person earning ₹1 lakh a month might be viewed as financially stable, but this doesn't tell the full story. True financial stability goes beyond the mere number on a paycheck. It also includes factors like assets—savings, investments, or real estate—as well as liabilities such as loans and debts. A person who lives within their means, saves money, and plans for the future is more financially stable than someone who earns more but spends recklessly and accumulates debt. For instance, someone earning ₹90,000 a month, yet saving and investing wisely, having good net assets can be far more secure financially than someone earning ₹1.5 lakh a month who lives paycheck-to-paycheck, potentially having more liabilities than assets. Real financial stability is about making smart, sustainable financial decisions that lay the foundation for stability, growth, and security in the future.

Marrying into a well-off or respected family does not guarantee a happy marriage.

The Right Way to Assess Financial Stability

True financial stability goes beyond income—it involves:

o   **Assets:** Savings, Financial Investments, Real estate, etc.

o   **Liabilities:** Loans, Debts, and EMIs.

o   **Spending vs. Saving Habits:** Is the person financially prudent, or do they live paycheck-to-paycheck?

o   **Financial Planning:** Does the person plan for the future, or only focus on short-term gains?

Example:

o   A person earning ₹90,000 a month with no debt and saving and investing wisely is more financially stable than someone earning ₹1.5 lakh but drowning in debt and not having investment habits.

Focusing solely on material stability—such as income, a nice house, or social status—when selecting a marriage partner can lead to emotionally disconnected unions. Despite having all the signs of financial security, many relationships fail when emotional compatibility and mutual respect are absent. For example, even with a house, car, and a stable job, couples may feel lonely and distant from one another. While money can provide comfort, it cannot replace emotional intimacy, shared values, or the deep connection that makes a marriage flourish. In some families, marriage has become a financial transaction rather than a partnership built on love and respect. Phrases like

"We gave a large dowry, so we expect her to adjust fully to the husband's family" or "He has a great job, so we'll overlook his bad temper"

are all too common. This transactional mindset distorts the true meaning of marriage, reducing it to an economic exchange rather than a chance to build a mutually supportive, soulful relationship. It places more importance on social status than on emotional well-being, and it creates imbalanced power dynamics where one partner feels superior because of their financial contributions. This imbalance can lead to resentment and a lack of true connection, making marriage more of a contract than a collaboration.

First Date? Who should pay the bill?

There's a widespread conversation among youngsters today around a simple but surprisingly contentious question: Who should pay for the first date? Should it be entirely the man's responsibility, or should the woman also contribute equally?

Many women argue that men should pay—suggesting that if a man can't pay for a date, how will he ever take care of a family? The belief is that "real men" pay the bills, and that it's their responsibility to cover such costs. On the other hand, many men feel that in an era where women are financially independent and proudly tag themselves as such, equality should also extend to dating, especially when money is involved.

Here's my view—one that considers both practicality and fairness.

If you're going on a first casual meet just to explore how you get along, then I believe both should pay equally. It doesn't matter who initiated the meeting—because at this stage, you're both figuring each other out. There's no commitment, no defined relationship, and certainly no foundation for assigning responsibility. Until things get serious and you're officially dating, there's no reason to expect one person—especially the man—to bear the full cost.

Also, when women take pride in being independent in every other aspect, why should this be an exception? Even for those who believe that men should handle financial responsibilities in a family, a first casual meet is far from building a family. This logic simply doesn't apply at such an early stage.

Moreover, in today's world where casual meets and first dates are increasingly common, there have been rising cases of financial exploitation—where individuals, unfortunately, go out not with the intent of forming a connection, but to gain something materially at someone else's expense. In this context, splitting the bill becomes not only fair but a safeguard against misuse.

That said, if a man insists on paying, that's a gesture and a generous one. But in that case, it's equally thoughtful for the woman to offer to split, pay fully, or contribute according to her financial comfort. Respect and equality must work both ways.

Real compatibility begins with shared values, not outdated expectations.

Wedding expenses: How much is too much?

In many cultures, weddings have become grand events often viewed as status symbols, with families spending extravagant amounts to host them. Weddings in India have increasingly become financial showpieces, often driven by societal comparisons, cultural prestige, and emotional sentiment. But beneath the glamour lies a critical truth—wedding expenses should be anchored to a clear, rational budget, ideally as a percentage of the total net worth of those involved. In most Indian families, parents shoulder the bulk of this financial responsibility, so their net worth and financial capacity must also be taken into account alongside that of the couple. The problem arises when budget decisions are made based on comparison, social pressure, or unreasonably high aspirations. This kind of financial mismanagement can leave lasting scars—sometimes plunging families into debt or compromising future goals. People often justify it with the phrase, *"You only get married once,"* but a few days of grandeur are not worth years of financial strain. It's important to remember weddings last for a few days, but life—and its financial realities—last for decades. Choosing mindfulness over extravagance is not just practical; it's wise.

It's common for families to take on significant debt to pull off an elaborate celebration, believing that the impression made will last a lifetime.

However, the harsh reality is that while the wedding may last for just a few days, typically 3 to 7 but its financial impact can last for many years.

The right approach is to set a wedding budget based on your financial situation, not societal pressure.

It's important to remember that no event, no matter how grand, should force you into debt. Taking loans to finance a wedding can create long-term financial stress, as the weight of that debt could overshadow the joy of the occasion. A balanced and thoughtful approach to wedding expenses ensures that the focus remains on the celebration, not the financial burden that follows.

Storyline 4

The Weight of Old Promises – Kusum and Dipesh's Dilemma

Kusum, a gifted fashion designer from a modest middle-class background, had always been a pillar of strength for her family. When her father took early retirement due to health issues, she stepped up—both emotionally and financially. Among her many responsibilities was the EMI for the family's new car, a vehicle used by her father, younger brother, and sister for daily commuting and errands. It was her silent way of saying: *"I've got this."*

But life changed after marriage. Kusum moved to another city to start a new life with Dipesh, a thoughtful and practical man. As they built their life together, new financial responsibilities naturally emerged—a home loan, shared expenses, and savings goals for the future. Dipesh, while respectful of Kusum's commitment to her family, brought up a concern during one of their monthly budgeting discussions:

Kusum stood at the window of their modest apartment in Pune, looking out blankly as evening lights flickered to life across the skyline. Dipesh was balancing the spreadsheet of their monthly expenses on the dining table, rubbing his temple.

Dipesh (gently): "Kusum… can we talk about something?"

She turned toward him, still holding the half-folded dupatta in her hand.

Dipesh: "The car EMI. It's… quite a hit on our monthly cash flow. Especially now with the house EMI and rising expenses."

Kusum (firmly): "I know. But I had committed to it. I bought that car for home—my home. I can't just back out because I'm married now."

Dipesh: "I understand. But you're not using the car anymore. You're here. Your brother and sister are using it daily, and both are earning now."

Kusum (a little sharper): "So what? That doesn't change the fact that it was my decision. I took it knowing what I was doing. This isn't about usage, Dipesh. It's about standing by my word. And just because I moved, doesn't mean that's not my home anymore."

Dipesh paused, letting her words hang in the silence.

Dipesh (calmly): "I'm not questioning your values, Kusum. I respect what you did—and what you continue to do for your family. But this isn't about abandoning them. It's about making room for *us* too. Things have changed. Don't you think we should adapt?"

Kusum didn't respond. That night, she stared at the ceiling long after Dipesh had fallen asleep. She replayed every moment—the joy of gifting that car, the sense of pride on her father's face, the excitement of her siblings taking it for a drive. It *was* still her home. But wasn't this her home too now?

A few days later, she called her siblings for a candid conversation.

Kusum (hesitantly): "Hey, I need to talk to you both about the car EMI. I've been thinking... I'm not using it anymore, and things are getting tighter here with the house EMI and other expenses."

Her brother instantly cut in.

Brother: "Di, you don't even have to explain. You've done more than enough. We should've taken it over earlier."

Sister (supportively): "Yes. And we've both started earning. We'll manage it together. It's time."

Kusum felt tears sting her eyes—not out of guilt or regret, but out of relief and growth. That night, she looked at Dipesh and said softly:

Kusum: "You know... I was holding on to something more emotional than financial. I think I was scared it would mean letting go of my home... my people. But you helped me see— letting go doesn't mean letting down."

Dipesh (smiling): "And standing by your word doesn't mean never changing it. Especially when you're not alone in carrying the weight anymore."

Kusum's story isn't just about one EMI. It's about the emotional weight of responsibility, the guilt we silently carry, and the difficulty of evolving old promises into new realities. Her journey shows that in a healthy marriage; partners must not only support one another—but also challenge each other to reassess what truly serves the present without dishonouring the past.

"Adaptation isn't betrayal, it's a form of love that includes both where you come from and where you're going."

Financials post Marriage

When it comes to financial compatibility, simply having individual financial stability is not enough in a marriage. How partners manage money together is crucial. Common disagreements arise when one partner is a saver while the other is a spender, or when they disagree on major purchases and investments. Financial incompatibility can surface in ways that create tension, such as one partner feeling burdened by the other's debts or disagreements over money being sent to extended family members. For example, one might say, "My wife spends so much on shopping that we can't save," or "My husband sends too much money to his family without discussing it with me."

Building financial compatibility requires open communication. Couples need to discuss their spending habits, savings goals, and how they want to manage finances such as joint or separate accounts. It's also essential to set clear boundaries: agree on how much financial support is reasonable for extended family and set limits on personal spending without feeling the need to micromanage. Prior to marriage, it's important to maintain financial independence, but also to establish an equal risk-return approach for big-ticket items like vacations or investments. Both partners should contribute equally or in proportion to their financial capacity. This open communication and mutual understanding can help prevent future conflicts and establish a foundation for financial harmony in the relationship.

In many cultures, the expectation is still that the man should be the main breadwinner. This traditional view puts a lot of pressure on men to earn more while expecting women to adjust their financial roles. However, today's world is changing. More women are becoming financially independent and focused on their careers. As a result, couples now talk openly about sharing financial responsibilities, challenging old ideas about who should provide and who should manage the home finances.

Over time, financial priorities in a marriage can change due to career shifts, unexpected setbacks, or life events such as having children. One partner might decide to leave a job to focus on raising kids, or a sudden job loss could impact the household income. These changes require both partners to be flexible and maintain clear communication about money matters.

Working together to adjust budgets and plan for new financial realities is essential for keeping the relationship stable and stress-free.

Money isn't just about numbers—it carries a lot of emotional weight in a marriage. Sometimes, the way money is managed can make one partner feel powerful or, conversely, insecure. For example, a partner who earns more might feel superior, while the one who earns less might feel undervalued.

The key to a happy financial relationship is emotional awareness. By openly discussing financial feelings and needs, couples can build a strong foundation where money serves as a tool for shared goals, not a source of conflict.

"

Every couple fights, but what often matters more than the conflict itself is how you handle it. Some go silent, others explode, some over-explain, and others walk away. These aren't just reactions; they're learned emotional habits. A relationship doesn't suffer because two people argue, it suffers when one keeps avoiding, the other keeps chasing, or neither knows how to repair.
Healthy conflict resolution means:
- ✓ Listening without defensiveness
- ✓ Validating the other's feelings even when you disagree
- ✓ Being solution-oriented instead of scoring emotional points

"The strength of a couple isn't seen in how peaceful they are, but in how safely they can disagree without breaking the bond."

Chapter 5

HEARTS IN THE AGE OF TECHNOLOGY: THE CHANGING RELATIONSHIP LANDSCAPE

Storyline 5

Akshit had everything going for him—a young, handsome doctor who had recently moved from his small hometown to the ever-awake city of Mumbai. He was in a long-distance relationship with Aarti, a sweet, grounded girl from back home. They had grown close over time, bonded by familiarity and shared roots. But the move to Mumbai brought with it new energy, new people, and a dating culture that was starkly different from what he had known.

At first, it was just innocent observation. The bustling cafés, art events, and hospital corridors were filled with independent, ambitious women who spoke freely and carried themselves with striking confidence. Mumbai had a pulse, and it beat differently. It wasn't long before Akshit, curious and caught in the rush of this new world, created a profile on a dating app. Naturally, he marked himself as single.

Soon, he was swiping through profiles, chatting with women, and meeting a few. One connection stood out—Neesha, a brilliant and effortlessly elegant architect. Their conversations were easy, their chemistry real. She had a magnetic personality, and Akshit was drawn in completely. They began spending more time together—coffee shops, late-night drives, walks by Marine Drive. And yet, through all of this, Aarti remained in the background. She kept texting, calling, trying to keep their connection alive from afar. But Akshit was drifting, emotionally detached, and lost in the charm of something new.

Despite how things looked on the outside, Akshit was living a carefully stitched lie. He managed to keep both women unaware of each other. Neesha didn't know about Aarti. Aarti didn't know about Neesha. It worked—until it didn't.

One Friday night, Akshit had planned to meet Neesha. She didn't respond for hours. He called her again and again. The silence drove him into frustration. That night, he ignored Aarti's calls too. Drunk and restless, he showed up at Neesha's apartment, only to find it locked and dark. No one answered. Around midnight, she texted: *"Was out of town for urgent family work. Sorry I couldn't pick up."*

But something had shifted.

The next two days felt distant. Neesha's tone was colder, her replies sparse. Akshit couldn't take the uncertainty. The following Saturday night, unable to hold back, he showed up at her place again. This time, someone opened the door—a man. Akshit stood frozen. Neesha walked into view, clearly shocked.

"What are you doing here?" she asked bluntly.

"I just wanted to talk. You've been avoiding me. Who is he?" Akshit snapped, unable to hide his irritation.

She paused, her face calm but stern.

"Akshit," she said, "we went out a few times. That doesn't mean I owe you exclusivity. We are not in a relationship. I don't do possessiveness. You knew what this was. Please don't come here again."

The door shut.

In that moment, the world Akshit had carefully built came crashing down. He had taken a chance at something new, without understanding its rules—or its cost.

Back in his hometown, Aarti could feel the change. She sensed the growing distance, the disinterest, the absence of warmth. One day, she simply stopped trying.

Akshit was left alone, confronted by two truths: That chasing excitement without honesty leaves behind guilt and regret. And that in a world where anyone can connect with anyone in an instant, meaningful connections are rare—and fragile.

Dating has evolved dramatically over the past few decades. From arranged marriages to online swipes, the way people meet, connect, and build relationships has been transformed by technology, changing social norms, and evolving career priorities. This chapter explores how modern dating culture, career orientation, and the influence of social media shape today's relationships, often leading to delays in marriage, frequent breakups, and new challenges in love and commitment.

Online it is!

In modern times, dating has transformed significantly from the traditional, linear progression of meeting through friends or family, engaging in courtship, and progressing to engagement and marriage. Today, the dating scene is characterized by its fluidity and non-linear nature, with stages ranging from casual chatting to serious, exclusive dating, and often ambiguous situationships. The advent of technology has played a pivotal role in this evolution, with online dating apps, social media direct messages, and virtual meetups expanding the way individuals connect. This technological influence has broadened the spectrum of choices for individuals, simultaneously introducing higher expectations and greater confusion about relationship norms.

In modern relationships, people often juggle multiple options, a habit that can develop after experiencing disloyalty or heartbreak.

To safeguard against potential pain in future, individuals may keep spare options, preventing them from fully committing to a new relationship and giving their 100%. When someone cannot give their full attention and effort, their partner may feel neglected, and they also start seeking attention elsewhere. This behaviour sets off a vicious cycle where neither partner is fully invested, leading to a continuous loop of dissatisfaction and emotional disconnection.

This vicious cycle of modern dating diminishes the quality of relationships, making true emotional connections rare and transforming serious commitment into a rarity. It underscores a profound shift in how relationships are viewed and valued, turning what could be meaningful emotional investments into superficial encounters that resemble a game more than a genuine connection.

- **Endless Options:** The prevalent "swipe culture" in dating apps offers an illusion of infinite choices for potential partners. This overwhelming array of options can lead to decision fatigue, where individuals find it difficult to make any decision at all, and commitment issues, as the fear of missing out on a potentially better option keeps them from fully committing to one person.

- **Superficial Connections:** Many relationships initiated via dating apps are based primarily on physical appearance or cleverly crafted bios, rather than on deeper, more substantial levels of compatibility. This surface-level assessment can lead to relationships that are less likely to endure the complexities of real-life challenges.
- **Validation Culture:** For some, dating apps and social media serve more as platforms for receiving validation and boosting self-esteem than for forming meaningful connections. This pursuit of validation can detract from the authenticity of interactions and hinder the development of genuine relationships.
- **Ghosting and Casual Flings:** The ease of access to potential partners has also popularized ghosting—ending a relationship by suddenly cutting off all communication without any explanation. Alongside this, the casual nature of connections formed on these platforms often leads to non-committal flings, further diminishing the emphasis on developing long-term, meaningful relationships. These trends contribute to a dating environment where emotional depth and accountability are often scarce.

The impact of social media on self-worth and relationships is profound and multifaceted, affecting how individuals perceive themselves and interact within their relationships:

- **Unrealistic Comparisons:** Social media platforms are rife with images and stories of "perfect couples," which can lead individuals to compare their own relationships to these idealized versions. Such comparisons often result in dissatisfaction with one's real-life relationships, as they may seem less exciting or fulfilling in contrast to the highly curated images seen online.

- **Pressure for Perfection:** There is a significant pressure on social media users to portray their relationships as flawless. This expectation can lead to the creation of inauthentic connections, where individuals are more concerned with maintaining an image rather than addressing the real dynamics and challenges in their relationship.

- **Post-Breakup Stalking:** Social media also enables individuals to keep tabs on their ex-partners, which can lead to prolonged emotional distress. The ability to constantly check on an ex's activities online can hinder the healing process, making it difficult to move on and forge new, healthy emotional attachments.

Breakups

In the landscape of modern dating, the occurrence of frequent breakups and the engagement in multiple relationships have become increasingly normalized. This shift is influenced by several factors:

- **Casual Dating Culture:** It is now common for individuals to date multiple partners before deciding to settle down. This approach allows for exploring various options but also leads to more frequent relationship terminations.

- **Higher Expectations:** With the vast array of choices available through dating platforms, people's standards for a suitable partner have increased. Consequently, relationships are often ended over minor issues that might have been overlooked in the past.

- **Shorter Attention Spans:** Influenced by the "on-demand" nature of social media and dating apps, people have grown more impatient with relationships. This impatience often manifests as a reluctance to work through challenges, leading to quicker breakups.

- **Fear of Missing Out (FOMO):** Even when committed, some individuals continue to wonder if there might be a better match out there. This fear can undermine current relationships, making it difficult to fully commit.

Tracking Partner's Location

I've never been fully comfortable with the idea of tracking someone's location, not because I think people shouldn't share things, but because I don't want to love someone out of surveillance. Love, to me, is about freedom, not monitoring.

If I'm sharing my location with my partner, I want it to come from mutual understanding like for travel safety or convenience not as a tool to manage suspicion. Because the moment I need to "check where they are" out of anxiety or doubt, I know the problem isn't in their location—it's in the relationship's foundation.

Trust isn't built with apps. It's built with conversations, consistency, and mutual respect. I don't want to be in a relationship where I'm tracked or where I'm tracking, I want to be in a relationship where I'm trusted and where I trust.

Pre-Marital

In contemporary society, pre-marital sex is increasingly common, particularly in urban and metropolitan settings, although cultural taboos continue to linger. This shift toward more liberal attitudes reflects a recognition that physical compatibility is crucial alongside emotional and intellectual connections. However, societal judgment persists, especially in conservative circles, leading to secrecy and guilt due to moral policing and cultural stigma.

As physical appearance and sexual chemistry often overshadow deeper compatibility in modern dating, this approach is fuelled by media portrayals of ideal bodies and relationships, the culture of instant gratification, and the need for social validation from being with an attractive partner. This emphasis on superficial traits tends to lead to disappointments as looks fade and sexual chemistry changes without a foundational emotional and value-based connection.

The casual dating culture has also fostered a fear of emotional vulnerability, with many people becoming guarded to protect themselves from potential hurt. This protective stance blocks deeper connections and leads to a perpetual cycle of shallow relationships and fear of commitment. Such dynamics often result in 'situationships'—informal and undefined relationships that lack commitment.

To cultivate more meaningful connections in the realm of modern dating, it is crucial to develop self-awareness about one's true desires, independent of societal pressures. Embracing emotional vulnerability, balancing expectations between physical attraction and emotional compatibility, and fostering open communication about boundaries and intentions from the outset are essential. These steps can help steer modern dating away from its superficial and transient tendencies towards more substantial and fulfilling relationships. The ongoing challenges such as commitment issues, emotional detachment, and the prioritization of career over relationships underline the complex landscape of modern romantic relationships.

Micro Cheatings

Micro-cheating is one of the most subtle, yet increasingly rampant threats to modern relationships. It includes small acts that may not look like outright infidelity—like flirtatious texting, emotionally leaning on someone outside the relationship, or engaging in secret conversations with romantic undertones. The ambiguity around what counts as "cheating" makes it harder to draw a clear line. But there is one simple filter:

if you were to share it with your partner, and it would hurt them or make them question your loyalty, then it's a form of emotional dishonesty.

Micro-cheating often slips under the radar—not because people intentionally wish to hurt their partner, but because they don't even realize they are doing it. The real danger lies in the habit it forms. These small, unchecked actions can slowly chip away at emotional closeness, creating invisible distance and subtle cracks in the relationship. Boundaries aren't always about restrictions—they're about protecting the emotional space you've built with your partner. Healthy couples define these boundaries not with control, but through clarity, openness, and mutual respect.

What makes micro-cheating dangerous is not just the act itself, but the habit it breeds. When repeated over time, these behaviours can reshape your emotional patterns, pulling you further from your partner without even realizing it. At first, it might feel harmless—"just a chat," "just a compliment," "just some harmless attention." But gradually, your mind learns to seek emotional validation outside the relationship, creating cracks in trust, weakening emotional intimacy, and distorting your sense of commitment. Over time, this can lead to a complete erosion of transparency and closeness, even when no physical boundary is crossed. The problem is not always what's done—but what it turns you into.

Unrealistic Expectations

Today's youth are often shaped by a steady stream of movies, reels, and curated social media moments that paint love and relationships as dreamy, effortless, and always exciting. While such content can be entertaining and even inspiring, it also sets the stage for unrealistic expectations—the belief that love should always feel magical, that partners must be flawless, and that life together will mirror cinematic perfection. Having dreams and goals are fine and sometimes you achieve thing in life which looked dreamy earlier.

But real life unfolds differently. Relationships involve effort, patience, emotional work, and moments of discomfort. The healthiest mindset is this: consume everything but stay grounded in reality. Enjoy the stories, the romance, the drama—but don't use them as your checklist for real love. Be hopeful but be real.

I often find myself standing at a strange crossroad, I want to be with someone, maybe even spend a lifetime with them… but I don't fully believe in the institution of marriage. Not in the traditional, ceremonial, "this is how it must be" kind of way. Part of me craves deep companionship, emotional intimacy, and shared goals. But another part resists the idea of being tied down by a social contract that feels more like an expectation than a personal choice. Maybe marriage doesn't have to be what others expect. Maybe it can be something we build………new, fluid, and honest.

"

Many people struggle to open up. They fear being judged, misunderstood, or used. In a world that romanticizes being "strong" and self-reliant, vulnerability is often mistaken for weakness.

But a deep relationship requires emotional availability, not just presence, but openness. The ability to say: *"I feel scared," "I'm unsure,"* *or "I need you."* The most intimate moments aren't physical; they're the ones where both people are emotionally naked and still feel safe.

"You can't expect to be fully loved while hiding half your soul. Vulnerability is the gateway to real intimacy."

Chapter 6

DYNAMICS OF DOMINANCE: POWER, RIGHTS, AND THE STRUGGLE WITHIN MARRIAGES

Storyline 1 Continued....

Ashish kept his word. He decided it was time to confront the silence that had built up in his home. He sat down with his parents one evening, gently trying to start the conversation. "Mom, Dad," he said, "I think we need to talk about everything that's been happening lately... between you, Aarti, and me."

They listened. Quietly, at first.

His father broke the silence. "Look, Ashish, we've always lived with one principle—spend less than you earn. Save enough. That's how we've kept this house running."

His mother added, "If we start spending unnecessarily, how will the house survive? Aarti doesn't understand this. She's always buying things—traveling, dressing up, getting gadgets."

Ashish stayed calm. "But she's not spending your money," he said firmly. "She's spending what she earns. She wasn't a part of this household earlier. She has her way of living—and she's not asking anything from us."

His mother's face tightened. "It's not just the money," she admitted. "I get tired doing everything at home. She doesn't help. Even if she's working, she's still a daughter-in-law of this house. There are responsibilities."

Ashish recognized the deeper truth in that moment. This wasn't only about money. It was about *roles*—what was expected, what was unspoken, and what was still rooted in generational beliefs.

"But that's not a fair expectation," he replied softly. "She works a full-time job too. Things have changed."

His parents didn't agree. "Look around," his father said. "All working women in our society still do household work. That's how families run. Why should we be any different?"

Ashish realized no one was being cruel—just deeply conditioned.

Still, he knew this wasn't sustainable.

That night, he called Aarti. They hadn't spoken properly since she left.

"I spoke to Mom and Dad," he said. "Tried to explain everything."

Aarti didn't sound surprised. "And?"

"They don't really get it. They still believe the old way of doing things is the only way."

She paused, then said what she had probably rehearsed in her mind for days.

"I don't want to fight every day. I don't want to live in a home where I feel judged for every choice I make—whether it's my clothes, my job, or even a phone I buy with my own money. I want peace, Ashish. I want space. Let's stay separately. Maybe some distance will help everyone breathe."

Ashish felt like a rope being pulled at both ends.

Now, he had a new dilemma:

- **Talk to his parents and ask for a separate arrangement**—risking emotional strain and possibly hurting them.

- Or **keep trying to convince Aarti** to return, hoping that with time, things at home would settle down on their own.

Both options came with emotional costs.

For someone who once laughed his way through life, this moment was painfully real. No jokes. No charm. Just choices. Heavy ones.

This is where the story of Ashish will pause again—right at the edge of the hardest decisions a person can face: when love, loyalty, and logic don't align.

Marriage is often perceived as a union built on love, respect, and equality, but the reality is that power dynamics play a significant role in shaping the health and longevity of the relationship. From decision-making authority to emotional leverage and societal gender roles, power struggles can strain even the strongest partnerships. This chapter explores the underlying power dynamics in marriages, how they manifest, and how couples can create a balanced, respectful, and empowering relationship.

Understanding Power Dynamics in Marriage

Power dynamics within a marriage encompass how decisions are made, who holds influence, and how conflicts are resolved.

Achieving a healthy balance of power is crucial for a harmonious relationship.

- **Healthy Power Balance**: In a balanced relationship, both partners feel their voices are heard and respected. They participate equally in decision-making processes, reflecting a partnership where emotional, financial, and household responsibilities are shared equitably. This balance fosters mutual respect and supports the relationship's long-term sustainability.

- **Unhealthy Power Imbalance**: An imbalance occurs when one partner consistently dominates decisions, often leading to emotional manipulation, control, or financial dependency. This can breed resentment and conflict, undermining the relationship's stability and the well-being of both partners. Recognizing and addressing these imbalances early is critical in preventing long-term dissatisfaction and discord.

Traditional Gender Roles and Power Imbalances

Traditional gender roles have long influenced marital dynamics, often dictating the responsibilities and expected behaviour of spouses based on their gender.

- **Cultural Expectations**: In many societies, men are traditionally seen as the primary providers and decision-makers, while women are expected to be nurturers and caretakers, primarily focusing on home and family management.

- **Problems with Rigid Roles**: These predefined roles can severely limit personal growth and lead to emotional disconnection within the marriage. Such restrictions not only prevent individuals from pursuing personal goals but can also lead to power imbalances that foster resentment and frustration.

- **Challenges for Non-Conforming Individuals**: Women who choose to focus on their careers or deviate from traditional caretaker roles often face societal judgment or pressure to conform. This external pressure can exacerbate internal conflicts within the marriage, potentially leading to emotional detachment and dissatisfaction.

Understanding and navigating these dynamics and cultural expectations are essential for fostering a relationship based on equality and mutual respect. Couples must engage in open and honest discussions about their expectations, roles, and the balance of power in their relationship to ensure both partners feel valued and empowered.

Emotional Power Struggles

Emotional power struggles in marriage can manifest subtly and insidiously, significantly affecting the relationship's dynamics and health.

- **Withholding Affection or Attention**: Using affection or attention as a form of punishment or control can deeply hurt the relationship, creating a dynamic where love and care are conditional.
- **Emotional Manipulation**: Tactics such as guilt, blame, or passive-aggressive behaviour are used to influence or control the partner's actions. This manipulation can deeply affect the emotional health of the relationship.
- **One-sided Emotional Labor**: When one partner consistently handles the bulk of emotional responsibilities—such as planning, nurturing, and conflict resolution—it can lead to an imbalance that burdens one partner disproportionately.

Over time, these struggles can lead to emotional disconnection and resentment, where one partner may feel undervalued or neglected. Addressing these issues through open communication and therapy can be crucial in re-establishing a healthy dynamic.

Financial Power Dynamics

Money is a significant factor in power dynamics within marriages, often influencing how power is distributed between partners.

- **Influences of Financial Dynamics**:

  - **Income Disparities**: Often, the partner who earns more may wield more decision-making authority, potentially leading to power imbalances.

  - **Financial Dependency**: Partners who are stay-at-home or earn less may feel vulnerable due to their financial dependency, affecting their autonomy and sense of control within the marriage.

- **Healthy Financial Dynamics**:

  - **Transparency**: Both partners should be fully aware of and involved in managing finances, including savings and spending habits.

  - **Joint Decision-Making**: Decisions about finances should be made together, ensuring that both voices are heard, regardless of who earns more.

  - **Valuing Contributions**: Recognizing that non-financial contributions, such as homemaking, child-rearing, and emotional support, are invaluable to the family's overall health and wellbeing.

Decision-Making Conflicts and Control

Conflicts often arise in areas where decisions impact both partners, including finances, children, career choices, and lifestyle.

- **Examples of Decision-Making Power Struggles**:

  - Unilateral decisions about significant expenses or investments can create conflict and resentment.

  - Disagreements over parenting styles, family traditions, or the extent of family involvement in personal matters.

  - Conflicts arising from differing preferences on social engagements, travel, or other lifestyle choices.

- **Strategies for Healthy Decision-Making**:

  - **Equal Participation**: Ensuring that both partners have an equal say in significant decisions, respecting each other's views and opinions.

  - **Compromise**: Finding a middle ground that respects both partners' wishes and values when disagreements arise.

  - **Clear Communication**: Regular discussions about expectations, needs, and the reasoning behind decisions are vital for maintaining clarity and understanding.

Navigating these dynamics thoughtfully and respectfully can help mitigate conflicts and enhance the health and longevity of the relationship, fostering a partnership based on equality and mutual respect.

The Challenges to Adjust in a New Family

Adjusting to a new family post-marriage is a significant transition, particularly for women, who often face intense pressure to conform to their husband's family dynamics. This adjustment involves more than just a change of residence; it encompasses adapting to entirely new sets of traditions, beliefs, and daily routines.

Women frequently move into their husband's family home, where they are expected to integrate into the existing family culture. This might include adopting different domestic roles, engaging with new familial rituals, and often, conforming to a set of expectations that can be vastly different from her own family's ways.

If the new family is particularly rigid or conservative, the woman may struggle with a sense of isolation or alienation. The lack of flexibility in the family's expectations can make it difficult for her to express her true self, leading to feelings of suppression and loneliness.

When problems arise, she turns to her husband for support. But if he sides with his family, it leads to emotional distress and a feeling of being trapped," highlights a critical aspect of these dynamics. The woman's primary support system in this new environment is often her husband. However, if he consistently aligns with his family's views over hers, it can create a significant emotional rift between the couple. This situation can leave the woman feeling unsupported and trapped, exacerbating feelings of isolation and distress.

To navigate these challenges, it is crucial for couples to establish strong communication lines where the feelings and perspectives of both partners are respected and considered. Husbands need to play a proactive role in bridging the gap between their wives and their families, ensuring that their spouses feel valued and supported. Furthermore, fostering an environment where new members can express their views and contribute to the family's culture can significantly ease the transition and promote healthier family dynamics.

When Parents Become a Burden on the Marriage

In many cultures, the influence of parents and extended family can play a significant role in a couple's life, sometimes leading to tension and conflict. Parents, often unintentionally, may impose their own beliefs, traditions, and experiences onto the newly married couple, which can strain the relationship.

After marriage, some parents continue to interfere, setting expectations on how the couple should live, work, and even raise children. They dictate rituals, traditions, and family dynamics, turning marriage into a struggle rather than a partnership.

- **Rigid Expectations on the Daughter-in-Law**: Parents, especially those from traditional backgrounds, might expect the daughter-in-law to conform strictly to their ways of managing a household. Statements like, "My wife did this, so my daughter-in-law should too," or "She must wake up early, handle all household work, and follow traditions," are indicative of rigid, predefined roles that leave little room for personal autonomy or modern partnership dynamics.

- **Micromanaging the Couple's Relationship**: Parents may also intrude into the personal decisions of the couple, such as their financial planning or family planning choices. Comments like, "Why are you going on a vacation so soon after marriage? Save money!" or "You should have kids within two years!" reflect an overreach into the couple's private life, which can create pressure and discord.

- **Control Over Family Rituals and Customs**: In many families, adherence to long-standing rituals and customs is expected. Demands such as, "Our family has always done pujas in this way; you must follow the same rituals," or "Marriage ceremonies should happen exactly as we did in the past," impose a continuity that might not resonate with the younger generation's views or beliefs.

The Role of Boundaries in Maintaining Balance

Healthy boundaries are critical for maintaining respect and individuality within a marriage. These boundaries help each partner retain their sense of self while contributing positively to the relationship.

Types of Boundaries:

- Personal Space: Each partner should have the freedom to pursue their personal interests and hobbies, ensuring they maintain their individuality and personal growth.
- Emotional Boundaries: It's important to recognize when to give space during conflicts to prevent escalation and allow for cooling down, which can lead to more constructive discussions later.
- Family Boundaries: Setting clear limits on how much family members can intervene in the couple's life is crucial.

This protects the couple's autonomy and prevents external influences from causing conflicts within the marriage.

Without appropriate boundaries, resentment can build, potentially leading to emotional distance. Additionally, over-dependence on one partner may arise, straining the relationship further.

Navigating Power Struggles Without Damaging the Relationship

Power struggles within a marriage are inevitable, but the manner in which couples handle these conflicts can define the overall health of their relationship. Strategies for Managing Power Struggles:

- Communicate Openly: Address issues honestly and directly, avoiding blame or passive aggression.
- Listen Actively: Make an effort to understand your partner's perspective, fostering a deeper emotional connection.
- Acknowledge Imbalances: Recognize and address any areas where one partner may feel disempowered, striving for a more balanced relationship.
- Seek Compromise: Aim for solutions that accommodate both partners' needs and desires.

Recognizing and Addressing Unhealthy Control

Controlling behaviours can severely impact a relationship's health and may escalate into emotional abuse if not addressed.

- Warning Signs:
  - If one partner consistently makes decisions unilaterally or uses emotional manipulation, guilt-

tripping, or threats to maintain control, these are significant red flags.

- o Isolation from friends, family, or social circles is another serious indicator of controlling behaviour.

- Actions to Take:

  - o Seeking support through counselling, reaching out to trusted friends, or professional help is crucial when control becomes abusive.

  - o Healthy relationships are founded on mutual respect, not dominance or control.

Promoting Equality and Partnership in Marriage

Equality in marriage encompasses a balance of responsibilities, respect, and emotional investment, ensuring that both partners feel valued and equally invested in the relationship's success.

- Key Elements of Equal Partnerships:

  - o Shared Responsibilities: Fair distribution of chores, parenting duties, financial responsibilities, and emotional labour.

  - o Mutual Respect: Both partners should value each other's opinions, needs, and desires.

  - o Emotional Safety: Ensuring that each partner feels heard, understood, and supported.

Empowering Each Other Within the Relationship

A strong marriage should be a supportive platform where both partners feel empowered to grow, evolve, and thrive.

- Fostering Growth and Individuality:

- o Encourage Personal Growth: Actively support each other's dreams, ambitions, and personal goals.

- o Celebrate Individuality: Recognize and appreciate each other's unique strengths and contributions to the relationship.

- o Foster Emotional Intimacy: Building trust through vulnerability, honesty, and shared experiences enriches the connection between partners.

A robust marriage is not about maintaining a power balance but about empowering each other to be the best versions of yourselves, thus enriching both the relationship and each individual's personal life.

Setting Boundaries with Family

Respectful boundaries are crucial for maintaining healthy family relationships while protecting the sanctity of the marriage. Here's how couples can set effective boundaries:

- **Joint Decisions**: Discuss as a couple the extent of family involvement that is comfortable for both, ensuring both partners are on the same page.
- **United Front**: Present a consistent and united stance when addressing boundary issues with parents or extended family.
- **Support Your Partner**: It's vital to stand up for your partner during familial conflicts, ensuring they feel supported and defended within the family dynamic.

By setting boundaries, couples can preserve their independence, making decisions based on their needs rather than familial pressure. Proper boundaries help ensure that family dynamics do not interfere with the couple's personal decisions and relationship harmony.

Healthy Discussion at the Male's Family End Before Marriage is Crucial

Addressing expectations and roles before marriage can significantly reduce conflicts:

- **Expectations of the Daughter-in-Law**: Clear conversations about what the family expects from the daughter-in-law can prevent misunderstandings.
- **Parental Involvement**: Discuss the degree of parents' involvement in daily decisions to ensure it aligns with the couple's expectations.
- **Financial and Household Responsibilities**: Clarify how these responsibilities will be shared and managed within the marriage.
- **Respect for Personal Space**: Ensure there is a mutual understanding that the couple's personal space will be respected.

These discussions help in setting clear boundaries from the beginning, thus preventing many potential conflicts, and ensuring a smoother transition into married life.

Parents Need to Adapt to Changing Mindsets

The dynamic of relationships and marriage has evolved significantly, necessitating a shift in parental mindsets:

Parents should strive to understand how relationships function today, recognizing that dynamics such as financial independence and shared responsibilities have altered how marriages work. Emphasize that modern marriages are built on companionship, not merely duty and obligation. Parents should aim for their child's happiness and well-being, rather than adhering rigidly to traditions or exerting control over the marriage.

Make a Marriage Friendly Environment

Creating a welcoming home environment is crucial for the new family member to feel comfortable and accepted:

- **Respect for Personal Space**: The new family member should feel free to express their opinions and live independently within the family unit.
- **Minimize Interference**: Parents should avoid micromanaging the couple's relationship, allowing them to nurture their bond.
- **Emotional Support Over Pressure**: The family should provide support rather than imposing responsibilities that might overwhelm the new member.
- **Adaptation Time**: Acknowledge that the new member needs time to adjust to the family culture, rather than expecting immediate conformity.

Growth and Adaptability in Relationships – Understanding Advice vs Acceptance vs Dominance

One of the common misunderstandings in relationships, especially in marriage, is mistaking advice or suggestions as a lack of acceptance. When in-laws or partners offer guidance, request changes, or encourage adjustments, it's natural to instantly feel defensive—*"They don't accept me for who I am."* But before reacting negatively, it's important to ask: Isn't this something you've already experienced throughout life?

Your parents, teachers, and friends have never accepted you exactly as you were—they've always encouraged you to learn, evolve, and try new things. As a child, you were constantly pushed to improve, to study, to develop better habits. As a teenager, your friends may have advised you to step out of your comfort zone, explore different perspectives, and grow in ways you never imagined. At 20, you were a different version of yourself than you are at 26. Haven't you changed over the years? Haven't you evolved based on experiences, exposure, and feedback from those around you?

So why does it suddenly feel different when it comes from a partner or in-laws? The issue isn't change itself—it's our perception of it. In friendships and early life experiences, change feels organic and self-directed. In relationships and marriage, it sometimes feels forced or imposed, triggering a sense of resistance. But not every piece of advice or suggestion means the other person is trying to erase your individuality—sometimes, it's simply a way of helping you navigate life together in a more harmonious way.

The key is differentiating between positive influence and control. If a partner or in-law is suggesting something that genuinely contributes to personal growth, shared happiness, or mutual understanding, being open to change isn't a weakness—it's emotional intelligence and adaptability. However, if change is demanded in ways that compromise core values, self-respect, or personal identity, then it's valid to stand firm. The goal isn't to be rigid or to conform blindly but to remain flexible in areas that allow for personal and relational growth.

Marriage, like life, is a journey of constant evolution. Adapting doesn't mean losing yourself—it means expanding your understanding of love, relationships, and personal growth. Instead of instantly reacting with resistance, ask yourself: *"Is this change something that could help me evolve, just as I have in other areas of life?"* If the answer is yes, then maybe, just maybe, growth isn't something to fear but to embrace.

"An important trait to look for in a partner is a problem-solving attitude, especially because daily life is filled with small, recurring challenges, be it home repairs, grocery purchases, preparing meals, managing mobility, or general maintenance and cleaning. A healthy approach is to address and resolve these issues efficiently, rather than allowing them to linger. Wherever possible, the goal should be to find long-term solutions, even if it involves spending money, if it leads to greater peace, convenience, and happiness."

"

People express and receive love in different ways, known as the five love languages:

- Words of affirmation
- Acts of service
- Quality time
- Physical touch
- Gifts/luxury

Problems arise when you're giving love the way you understand it, not the way your partner feels it.
For example, one partner may say "I love you" daily, while the other just wants help with chores to feel loved. This mismatch leads to emotional confusion and unmet needs, not because love is missing, but because it's being lost in translation.

"Loving someone isn't just about giving, it's about giving in the language they hear."

Chapter 7

LOVE AND AMBITION: THE CAREER-MARRIAGE BALANCING

In the modern world, career ambitions and personal relationships often collide, creating challenges for individuals trying to balance love and professional growth. This chapter explores how career orientation, personal goals, and the pressure to settle down intersect, leading to delayed marriages, strained relationships, and evolving dynamics in love and commitment.

The Rise of Career-First Mindsets

In contemporary urban settings, career ambitions increasingly take precedence, with many prioritizing education, financial stability, and personal growth before even considering marriage. The common mantra, "I need to be settled in my career before I think about marriage," encapsulates this shift. Reasons for this career-first approach include a desire for financial security, ensuring one can support themselves and a future family, and personal fulfilment, with individuals seeking to achieve career milestones before committing to someone else. Additionally, there's a pervasive fear that marriage might limit personal freedom or career opportunities.

Is Career important?

In today's society, many young adults are placing a greater emphasis on their career ambitions, which often leads to delayed marriages. Key reasons for this trend include a desire for financial stability before settling down, fear that marriage could restrict personal and professional growth, and a pursuit of independence that encourages experiencing life fully before making long-term commitments.

This shift in priorities has a significant impact on relationships. Romantic relationships are increasingly becoming more casual and exploratory, with less focus on long-term commitment. As individuals prioritize their careers, emotional connections often take a back seat, which can lead to breakups when there is a clash in priorities. Additionally, a prevalent commitment phobia has emerged, where people hesitate to engage deeply in relationships out of fear that it may hinder their personal growth and career progress.

There is a growing consensus among many individuals, particularly men, that achieving personal success and establishing self-recognition are crucial before finding the right partner. Belief that the female counterpart always gets attracted to money and success.

This has also some implications which may motivate men to keep working and putting efforts towards their goals. This belief stems from the idea that self-worth and success not only enhance one's attractiveness as a partner but also provide a stable foundation for entering a relationship. This perspective emphasizes the importance of being secure in one's own identity and accomplishments, irrespective of whom one chooses to be with.

How Career Orientation Delays Marriage and Relationships

Long working hours, demanding jobs, and frequent career shifts often leave little time for personal relationships. Commonly heard phrases like, "I'm too busy to date seriously right now," underscore this reality. The challenges are compounded by frequent relocations for work, which can destabilize relationships. Moreover, a heavy focus on career can lead to emotional exhaustion, leaving little energy for love and intimacy, thereby delaying marriage into the late 30s or 40s, fostering casual dating, and leading to frequent breakups and shallow connections.

The Internal Conflict: Love vs. Ambition

Many face an internal conflict between the desire for love and the pursuit of career goals. This tug-of-war often manifests as guilt over prioritizing work over relationships or fear of regret from potentially ending up lonely due to a singular focus on career. Relationships can strain under the weight of career ambitions dominating the dynamics, leading to neglected partners who may feel secondary to their significant other's professional life.

When Partners Have Unequal Career Ambitions

Relationship conflicts frequently arise when partners have different levels of ambition or focus on their careers. Statements like, "She's so career-driven, and I feel left behind," or "He works so much that I feel like I'm not a priority," are common in such dynamics. Challenges include power dynamics, where one partner earning significantly more may lead to control issues or feelings of inadequacy, conflicts over time management, and tough decisions about the future when career goals differ, such as one partner needing to relocate for work.

The Career-Marriage Crossroads: When to Settle Down?

Many delays marriage, waiting for the "perfect time" when they are financially stable or have reached certain career milestones. However, life's unpredictability means there's rarely a "perfect" moment to get married. Important questions at this crossroads include whether one is delaying marriage for valid reasons or using their career as an excuse to avoid commitment, whether it's possible to balance love and ambition, and if both partners are supportive of each other's career goals.

The Fear of Love Becoming a Distraction

Some fear that engaging in a relationship might distract them from their career ambitions. While this concern is valid, healthy relationships can actually enhance personal growth rather than hinder it. A supportive partner can provide emotional stability and motivation, and emotional fulfilment from a relationship can boost productivity and creativity at work.

Balancing Love and Ambition: Is It Possible?

Balancing love and ambition is feasible, but it requires conscious effort and effective communication. Strategies for maintaining this balance include open discussion about career and personal goals, mutual support where partners celebrate each other's successes and help through failures, careful management of time to ensure quality moments together, and flexibility to adjust plans to support each other's needs.

When Career Ambition Leads to Relationship Strain

Warning signs of career ambition leading to relationship strain include one partner feeling neglected, emotional distance due to lack of quality time together, and resentment from one partner sacrificing their ambitions for the other. Solutions involve regular emotional check-ins, setting clear boundaries between work and personal life, and making time for shared experiences that strengthen the bond.

The Importance of Shared Values Over Shared Careers

It is not necessary for partners to have similar career ambitions; more crucial are shared values.

Questions like, "Do we both value personal growth and mutual support?" and "Are we aligned on how we view success and fulfilment?" help determine long-term compatibility. For instance, a high-powered executive and a creative artist can have a successful relationship if they respect and support each other's aspirations.

Love and Ambition Can Coexist

The idea that love and ambition cannot coexist is a myth. With proper communication, respect, and flexibility, couples can grow both individually and together, fostering fulfilling relationships where both partners feel empowered to pursue their ambitions while nurturing their emotional connection.

"The basic nature of relationship is boredom , not excitement all the time. Someone seeking sensation and excitement all the time may find difficult to stay put."

Chapter 8

BREAKING BONDS: DIVORCE, RELATIONSHIP CHANGES, AND FALLING OUT OF LOVE

Divorce and separation have long been viewed as failures or taboos in many cultures, especially in societies where marriage is seen as a lifelong commitment. However, as relationship dynamics evolve, so does the understanding of divorce—not merely as a breakdown but as an opportunity for self-discovery, healing, and growth. This chapter explores the emotional, social, and psychological complexities of divorce, the stigma surrounding it, and how individuals can redefine their views on love, commitment, and personal fulfilment after a failed marriage.

Emotions around Marriage struggle

When problems arise in a marriage, many individuals instinctively turn to their parents for help. They hope that their parents will listen without judgment, understand the emotional pain they are going through, and offer comfort and practical advice. In their eyes, parental support should provide a safe space where the burdens of marital conflicts can be shared and managed together.

However, the reality is often quite different. Instead of receiving genuine empathy, many people find that their parents tend to downplay the issues. Common responses like,

"It happens in all marriages, don't overthink it," or "Just adjust, things will get better with time,"

leave the person feeling invalidated. Rather than addressing the deep emotional hurt, these remarks suggest that the problem is minor or that the individual should simply endure the situation. This lack of meaningful support only adds to the strain on the marriage.

There are several reasons why parents react in this way. Often, parents find it hard to accept that their child is unhappy in their marriage, as it reflects on the decision they made when they approved the match. Additionally, many parents fear the societal repercussions of speaking openly about marital problems, worrying about what others might say. Their own upbringing, steeped in the values of endurance and sacrifice, leads them to believe that any marital challenge should be met with quiet adjustment rather than confrontation.

For the person seeking help, this dismissive response from parents can have a profound emotional impact. The expectation of support turns into a feeling of isolation and disappointment, as the lack of validation makes them feel alone in their struggle. Over time, this can erode trust in the parent-child relationship, making it difficult for the individual to open up about their challenges in the future. The cumulative effect of such responses often results in lingering resentment, not only toward the marriage but also toward the very people they expected to be their refuge.

A more compassionate and effective approach for parents is to listen first and advise later. It is important for parents to acknowledge the pain their child is feeling, saying something as simple as, "I understand that this is really tough for you." Instead of immediately pushing for endurance or suggesting that the situation will improve on its own, parents should encourage a thoughtful conversation about what might help alleviate the pain. Asking gentle questions like, "What do you think will make things better?" or "Would you like us to help you talk to your partner?" can provide the support needed to navigate the conflict. Such responses validate the child's feelings and empower them to make decisions that are best for their well-being.

In essence, when marital problems arise, the natural need for parental support is met with denial and dismissal, often driven by fear of societal judgment and outdated values of endurance. This not only leaves the individual feeling isolated and misunderstood but also weakens the trust in the parent-child relationship. By choosing to listen and validate rather than judge or dismiss, parents can offer a much-needed refuge, helping their children move forward with strength and clarity in their relationships.

Navigating Breakups and Divorce

Failure, whether in relationships, marriage, or love itself, is often seen as something to be ashamed of. However, every heartbreak, every failed relationship, and even every divorce teaches valuable lessons about what we truly need, who we are, and what we should never compromise on.

Resilience in love means learning from loss without letting it define us, it means carrying hope forward rather than the weight of past wounds.

Understanding divorce can be seen not as a failure, but as the natural end of a chapter that no longer benefits either partner. Often, society frames divorce as a personal failure, yet not all marriages are meant to last forever. Some relationships teach valuable lessons and guide us toward self-discovery. Many couples part ways because of issues like a lack of emotional or sexual compatibility, constant conflicts that they cannot resolve, or even instances of infidelity and breaches of trust. Sometimes, the reason is simply that both individuals grow apart as their goals, values, and interests evolve. In these cases, divorce is not about assigning blame but about recognizing that two people are taking different paths in life.

The emotional journey of separation is complex and varied. Divorce often triggers a mix of feelings such as grief, anger, guilt, relief, and confusion. Initially, many people find themselves in denial, struggling to accept that the relationship has come to an end. This may be followed by anger, where feelings of resentment—toward the partner, oneself, or the situation—take hold. As individuals try to bargain, they might hold on to the hope of fixing things, even when it is no longer healthy. This phase usually gives way to sadness, as one grieves the loss of the relationship and the future that was imagined together.

Ultimately, with time, acceptance begins to emerge, allowing for the focus to shift toward healing and moving forward. It is important to understand that experiencing a range of emotions is completely normal; allowing oneself the time to grieve is a crucial step in the path to healing.

Divorce in many cultures comes with a heavy social stigma. People often make harsh judgments, saying things like,

"She couldn't keep her marriage together" or "He must have done something terrible."

This stigma is compounded by double standards—women, in particular, face more criticism after a divorce, with their independence and dating lives scrutinized more than their male counterparts. At family gatherings, pressure mounts as relatives and friends question the decision to divorce, urging individuals to stay in unhappy marriages simply to avoid shame. Breaking this stigma requires recognizing that choosing personal happiness and self-respect over societal expectations is a brave and valid decision, and that divorce can mark the end of one chapter rather than a personal failure.

Divorce also has a profound impact on self-identity. When a marriage ends, it can lead to painful self-doubt, with questions like, "Am I unlovable?" or "What did I do wrong?" echoing in one's mind and worries about finding love again can be overwhelming. Rebuilding self-identity after divorce involves practicing self-compassion and understanding that relationships can fail for many reasons, most of which do not reflect one's worth.

Divorce becomes even more complex when children are involved. In these situations, the main focus should shift to creating a stable and loving environment for the child. Healthy co-parenting is key—both ex-partners need to maintain open, respectful communication and work together to prioritize the child's emotional well-being over their personal conflicts. Establishing clear boundaries and a detailed parenting plan can help reduce stress and ensure consistency for the child. It's also important to manage extended family dynamics by setting firm limits on interference and by educating the children about the changes in a way that is both age-appropriate and sensitive to their feelings.

lingering scars and Generalization

When a relationship fails—especially one where deep emotional investment was made—it often leaves behind lingering scars: disappointment, betrayal, anger, or grief. While such experiences can offer valuable lessons, they can also distort our ability to think rationally about love and relationships moving forward.

People often develop sweeping generalizations after heartbreak, thinking things like,

"All men are emotionally unavailable," or "Women only care about money."

These thoughts, though born out of pain, act as mental barriers, blocking any healthy emotional connection that might follow. The danger lies in projecting one bad experience onto all future possibilities. This leads to a paradox: you desire companionship, yet you're guarded, sceptical, or hyper-alert, expecting the worst even when someone is showing genuine care. For instance, you may meet someone kind and honest, but your past experience with manipulation may make you search for red flags that don't exist, ultimately sabotaging the potential of a meaningful relationship. To truly move forward, one must let go of these distortions and see each new person as an individual—not a reflection of a painful past.

Professional help, such as therapy or counselling, can be invaluable in processing these emotions and rebuilding trust. Forgiveness, especially forgiving oneself, plays a crucial role in letting go of the past. By releasing old hurts, individuals open themselves up to new beginnings and healthier, more fulfilling relationships.

Dating after divorce can bring a mix of excitement, fear, and hope. Many face challenges such as the fear of repeating past mistakes, difficulty trusting someone new, and pressure from family or society to "settle down" quickly. The best approach is to take time to heal and rebuild self-confidence before entering another relationship. Being open about your past, without dwelling on it, allows you to learn from previous experiences and set clear boundaries for what you need now. With patience and honest communication, dating after divorce can become a refreshing opportunity to rediscover love on your own terms.

Divorce offers a unique opportunity to reassess what love, and commitment mean to you.

After ending a marriage, many people begin to ask themselves, "What does love mean to me now?" and "What kind of partner do I want moving forward?" This period of reflection often leads to a deeper understanding of personal values and desires, paving the way for healthier, more balanced relationships in the future. Instead of viewing divorce as the end of love, it becomes a chance to start a new, finding a connection that truly aligns with who you have become.

Not everyone who goes through a divorce feels the need to jump into a new relationship right away. For some, singlehood is a fulfilling and enriching choice.

It provides the space to rediscover personal passions, nurture friendships, and focus on personal growth that may have been set aside during marriage. Embracing singlehood allows you to develop emotional independence and the freedom to explore new opportunities without external constraints. Rather than seeing being single as a void that needs filling, it can be celebrated as a period of self-discovery and empowerment.

Resilience is the cornerstone of healing and moving forward after divorce. It means acknowledging the pain of a broken chapter without letting it define your entire life. With resilience, you learn to take valuable lessons from the past while holding onto hope for a better future. This inner strength helps you rebuild your self-identity, approach life with optimism, and face new challenges with confidence. While divorce marks the end of one chapter, it opens the door to rewriting your story with renewed strength, self-love, and the courage to embrace new beginnings.

Healing After Heartbreak: The Journey Back to Self

Failure—whether in love, marriage, or any other part of life—is often viewed as something shameful. We internalize it, label ourselves as broken, and quietly carry guilt, regret, or resentment. But in truth, every heartbreak, every failed relationship, and even every painful divorce holds within it a lesson—sometimes even a revelation. These experiences teach us what we truly need, who we really are, and what we should never again compromise on. The loss hurts, but it also clears the space for growth.

Resilience in love doesn't mean becoming indifferent or cold— it means choosing to carry hope instead of old wounds. Whether it's a breakup, a failed career move, a financial loss, or a health setback, resilience is the quiet force that gets you back up when everything inside you feels like giving up. Getting back on track is an underrated kind of courage, one that doesn't always show in social media posts or dramatic declarations, but in the everyday effort to show up for yourself again. The strongest people aren't the ones who never fall—but those who come out of the darkness with clarity, fire, and softness all at once.

Healing, in its truest form, is not just forgetting a person or a painful memory—it's reclaiming yourself. It's rebuilding your confidence, restoring your emotional balance, and reigniting a sense of direction in life. It is about starting to love yourself again—fully, deeply, without waiting for external approval. Because when you genuinely love yourself, you stop chasing love that is built on validation and fear.

So how do you start loving yourself again?

- Make fundamental lifestyle shifts—nourish your body, rest your mind, get moving, get sleeping, eat with care.

- Reconnect with your purpose—find something meaningful to work toward and then let passion flow through that purpose.

- Seek wisdom—whether from books, nature, professionals, or simply life itself. When you tune into the universe with the right questions, answers begin to show up.

- Create joy in solitude—learn to enjoy your own company again, without feeling incomplete.

- Forgive yourself and others—not for their sake, but to free your own energy for what comes next.

At the heart of healing lies one eternal truth:

No matter what happens, never stop loving yourself. It is the only constant that keeps you going when everything else feels lost.

"When you're overly attached, your self-worth starts depending on the other person's moods, actions, or validation. You lose perspective. Detachment is about maintaining love without losing yourself in it. It is being close but not enmeshed. Present but not possessed."

"Healing does not rush you. It simply waits, waits for you to stop clinging to the narrative of what was lost and start believing again in what could still be possible."

Chapter 9

THE SOCIAL MEDIA ILLUSION – MARRIAGE AS A PERFORMANCE

In today's digital age, social media has transformed how we perceive relationships and marriage. Platforms like Instagram, Facebook, and YouTube have become public stages where couples showcase their love stories, grand gestures, and picture-perfect moments. While social media allows for connection and celebration, it has also created a distorted reality, where marriages are often curated for an audience rather than nurtured privately. This chapter explores how social media influences relationships, creates unrealistic expectations, and turns love into a performance rather than a personal journey.

"Couples post the perfect photo but never the argument they had five minutes before."

In today's digital age, social media is a double-edged sword, beautifully showcasing life's peak moments yet silently shaping unrealistic expectations about relationships. Here's a deeper dive into the nuances of this phenomenon:

- **Selective Sharing:** Social media is akin to a highlight reel where only the best plays are shown. What gets posted are vacations under exotic sunsets, surprise birthday parties, and anniversary celebrations. This selective sharing contributes to a skewed perception of continuous joy and unending romance, overshadowing the reality that relationships also involve mundane or challenging moments.

- **Impact on Self-Esteem:** Constant exposure to these idealized images can lead viewers to question the quality of their own relationships. This comparison trap can lead to feelings of inadequacy or dissatisfaction, with thoughts like, "Their life seems perfect! Why doesn't mine look like that?" Such comparisons can erode self-esteem and create discontentment with one's real-life circumstances.

- **Unrealistic Relationship Goals:** The barrage of perfect moments can set a high bar for what relationships should look like. Followers might believe that unless their own relationships mirror this perfection, something must be amiss. This can pressure individuals to mimic these displays, often forcing moments to appear perfect rather than allowing them to unfold naturally.

- **The Hidden Truth:** Behind every picture-perfect post often lies untold stories of struggle and normalcy. Real relationships involve compromise, conflict resolution, and growth through everyday challenges—none of which tend to make the cut for social media glamorization. Acknowledging this can help recalibrate one's expectations and appreciate the beauty in the ordinary.

Social Media Comparisons and Relationship Dissatisfaction

The pervasive nature of social media often paints a portrait of ideal relationships that can lead to destructive comparisons and dissatisfaction. Here's how this dynamic unfolds:

- **Unhealthy Comparisons:** Regular exposure to "perfect" relationships on platforms like Instagram or Facebook can prompt detrimental comparisons. Statements such as "Why doesn't my partner plan surprises like that?" or "Their life seems so exciting—ours feels boring in comparison," are common. These comparisons can skew perceptions of what a healthy relationship looks like, overshadowing the unique aspects of personal interactions.

- **Self-doubt and Insecurity:** Individuals may begin to doubt their relationship's worth if it doesn't resemble those seen online, leading to feelings of insecurity.

- **Resentment:** There can be a build-up of frustration or resentment towards a partner who is seen as not living up to these unrealistic standards.

- **Misplaced Metrics:** Couples might start evaluating the success of their relationship based on the amount of social media validation they receive instead of the strength of their actual connection.

Social media is a curated display, not a mirror of daily life.

The Rise of "Couple Goals" Culture

Social media has given rise to the "couple goals" phenomenon, where relationships are often showcased as benchmarks of perfection. Here's a deeper look:

Idealized Standards: Posts often feature matching outfits on vacations, over-the-top anniversary celebrations, or perfectly staged candid moments. These depictions foster a belief that love should always be thrilling, romantic, and effortless.

Reality Check: When personal experiences don't align with these polished standards, it can lead to disillusionment and dissatisfaction. The constant portrayal of an idealized relationship can distort one's expectations, making the normal ebbs and flows of a relationship seem inadequate.

Recognizing the staged nature of "couple goals" can help individuals maintain realistic expectations about relationships and value genuine interactions over fabricated displays.

Social Media and Relationship Conflicts

Social media, while connecting the world, often introduces unique challenges that can stir conflicts within romantic relationships. Here are some common issues couples face:

- **Disagreements on Sharing:** Couples may argue over what is appropriate to share publicly, leading to disagreements and discomfort.

- **Online Interactions:** Jealousy can surface over interactions with others online, such as likes, comments, or direct messages. Questions like "Who is this person always commenting on your photos?" reflect underlying insecurities.

- **Neglect Over Digital Presence:** If one partner frequently prioritizes their social media interactions over direct communication, it can lead to feelings of neglect and resentment.

Navigating these issues requires clear communication and understanding the emotional impact of online behaviours on relationships. Beyond affecting ongoing relationships, social media can also exacerbate the difficulties associated with breakups and divorces.

Prolonged Emotional Pain: Continuous exposure to an ex-partner's social media activities can hinder emotional recovery after a breakup.

Post-Breakup Performance: Social media can become a platform for individuals to showcase their recovery, often posting images that may not truly reflect their inner state.

Public Scrutiny: Breakups that play out publicly on social media can lead to unwanted gossip, judgment, and additional emotional stress.

Creating Healthy Boundaries with Social Media

To foster a healthy relationship in an era dominated by digital interactions, couples should consider setting clear social media boundaries:

Communication About Online Sharing: Discuss and agree on what feels comfortable to share online, respecting each other's privacy and feelings.

Limiting Comparisons: Remember that social media is not a full representation of life but a compilation of highlights.

Valuing Authentic Moments: Prioritize genuine experiences over capturing and posting them. This focus helps in building deeper connections.

Scheduled Offline Time: Regularly unplugging from social media can significantly benefit relationship quality by allowing partners to focus on each other without distractions.

Implementing these strategies can enhance intimacy and understanding, keeping the relationship grounded in reality rather than virtual perception.

In a world where online personas can overshadow real personalities, cultivating authentic relationships is key:

Focus on Genuine Intimacy: Building emotional intimacy without the influence of external validation fosters stronger, more resilient relationships.

Value Private Moments: Real, unshared moments of connection—be it a quiet conversation or a shared laugh—often mean more than any online post.

Encourage Real Interactions: Make an effort to engage in activities that foster closeness and genuine joy, beyond the digital gaze.

By prioritizing true intimacy over online appearances, couples can develop a robust foundation that withstands the challenges of the digital age.

"While dating, people often get into a mode of asking questions because they want to understand someone quickly. But you can't truly know a person in a jiffy, it takes time, patience, and shared experiences. While asking general questions can be a good starting point, the deeper understanding comes through meaningful conversations and careful observation. At the same time, it's important not to stretch the process endlessly. Striking a balance between letting things flow naturally and gathering clarity is key to genuinely knowing someone."

"Everyone would like to engage with the person who is happy and full of life and not someone who is annoyed and angry all the time. So, be full of life and you will attract right people in your life."

Chapter 10

THE MARRIAGE ILLUSION – A SOCIALLY CRAFTED REALITY

Marriage has long been seen as the ultimate life milestone—a symbol of stability, success, and fulfilment. However, much of what society portrays as the "ideal marriage" is a carefully constructed illusion, shaped by cultural expectations, traditions, and social narratives. People are led to believe that marriage is the natural and inevitable path to happiness, yet many enter it for the wrong reasons or with unrealistic expectations. When the reality of marriage doesn't align with these expectations, disappointment and disillusionment often follow.

The Social Construct of Marriage

Marriage is more than just a personal commitment—it is deeply rooted in societal structures and historical traditions. Historically, marriages were about alliances, wealth transfer, and family legacies, rather than love and companionship. Over time, as cultures evolved, marriage became romanticized - framed as the ultimate act of love and commitment.

However, despite the modernization of relationships, societal expectations around marriage remain deeply embedded. Many people still view it as a marker of success and social respectability, leading to immense pressure to conform. As a result, individuals often focus more on the act of getting married than on whether they are choosing the right partner or if marriage is truly the right path for them.

The Illusion of the "Perfect Marriage"

Movies, books, and social media have conditioned people to believe in the fantasy of a perfect marriage—a lifelong honeymoon filled with passion, companionship, and unwavering support. The common narrative suggests that once you meet "The One," everything will fall into place, and happiness will follow effortlessly.

This illusion creates unrealistic expectations, where people assume their partner should be their best friend, lover, therapist, and life coach all in one. However, when conflicts arise, as they inevitably do in any relationship, couples often feel disillusioned, believing something must be inherently wrong with their marriage. In reality, marriage—like any partnership—requires ongoing effort, adaptability, and mutual understanding. It is not about finding perfection but about creating a dynamic that works for both individuals.

The Pressure to Marry – The "When Will You Settle Down?" Question

In many cultures, especially in India, marriage is still considered a non-negotiable life event. Family, friends, and society often pressure individuals with constant questions:

- *"When are you getting married?"*

- *"What are you waiting for?"*

- *"Don't you want to settle down?"*

This pressure is even more intense for women, where age becomes a factor in perceived marriageability. As people watch their peers get married, they may feel a sense of urgency or fear of missing out, pushing them toward marriage before they are emotionally or mentally ready. Many prioritize external checklists—such as job status, financial stability, and physical appearance—over deeper emotional compatibility, leading to mismatched relationships and eventual dissatisfaction.

Marriage as a Transaction – The Materialistic Lens

Despite modern ideas of romance, marriage is still treated as a financial and social transaction in many societies. Families assess wealth, education, social status, and even dowry in arranged marriages, often prioritizing these factors over genuine emotional compatibility.

This transactional approach leads to various issues:

- Emotional disconnect: When marriage is based on social gain rather than emotional connection, intimacy suffers.

- Power imbalances: If one partner has more financial control, it can create dependency, control issues, and resentment.

- Superficial stability: A marriage may look perfect on the outside but lack trust, emotional intimacy, and real companionship.

Marriages that seem "perfect on paper" often turn out to be emotionally unfulfilling, highlighting the need to prioritize connection over external status.

The "Tick-the-Box" Mentality in Choosing Partners

Modern dating and arranged marriages often follow a checklist approach—partners are selected based on a set of predefined criteria rather than personal compatibility.

- *"Good job? Check."*

- *"Comes from a respectable family? Check."*

- *"Attractive? Check."*

The problem with this approach is that emotional compatibility, shared values, and communication often don't make the checklist. Many individuals end up with partners who fit societal standards but lack intellectual or emotional alignment. Over time, they realize that choosing a life partner based on external attributes rather than deep connection leads to emotional dissatisfaction and, in some cases, regret.

The Fear of Being Single – Choosing Marriage for the Wrong Reasons

One of the most common reasons people rush into marriage is the fear of being alone or being judged by society.

- *"Everyone around me is getting married—I should be too."*

- *"If I don't marry soon, people will think something is wrong with me."*

Choosing marriage out of fear rather than genuine desire often leads to long-term dissatisfaction. Partners may feel:

- Emotionally disconnected because they entered the marriage without deep compatibility.

- Trapped in a relationship that doesn't align with their values or aspirations.

- Resentful of societal expectations that forced them into an unhappy commitment.

A fulfilling relationship should be based on love, trust, and shared goals, not fear or societal timelines.

The Ritualization of Marriage – The Grand Celebration Over the Relationship

In many cultures, weddings have become lavish spectacles, sometimes overshadowing the actual relationship. Families spend enormous amounts of money to showcase wealth and social status, often prioritizing the wedding day over the long-term health of the marriage itself.

This leads to:

- Post-wedding blues: Couples realize they spent more time planning the wedding than preparing for marriage.

- Unnecessary financial stress: Huge expenses for temporary grandeur rather than long-term security.

- Emotional disconnect: The focus shifts from the relationship to how it appears to others.

A wedding is a single day, but marriage is a lifelong partnership. Investing time and effort into building a strong foundation is far more important than planning the perfect event.

The Disillusionment After Marriage – "Is This It?"

Many individuals experience disillusionment post-marriage when reality doesn't match the promises they were led to believe. Common realizations are:

- Love doesn't automatically solve all problems.

- Daily life involves mundane tasks, responsibilities, and compromises.

- Emotional connection requires continuous effort, not just initial chemistry.

This can lead to feelings of:

- Dissatisfaction—wondering if they made the right choice.

- Boredom—realizing that marriage isn't an endless romantic adventure.

- Regret—if they entered marriage for the wrong reasons.

Understanding that marriage is a dynamic journey, not a fairy tale, helps individuals build resilience and maintain long-term happiness.

Redefining Marriage – From Social Obligation to Personal Choice

To break free from the marriage illusion, individuals must redefine what marriage means to them personally. Instead of following a template set by society, family, or tradition, people should ask themselves:

- *"Do I want marriage because it aligns with my values or because society expects it?"*

- *"What kind of partnership would truly fulfil me?"*

- *"Can I find happiness outside of traditional marriage structures?"*

Shifting the focus from external validation to personal fulfilment allows people to make conscious, meaningful choices about love and commitment.

Choosing Authenticity Over Illusion

The healthiest marriages are those built on:

- Mutual respect and understanding.

- Emotional intimacy and shared values.

- Personal choice, not societal pressure.

Marriage shouldn't be about fitting into a Mold—it should be about creating a partnership that reflects who you truly are and what you genuinely desire. Whether one chooses to marry or not, the ultimate goal should always be personal fulfilment, happiness, and authenticity.

The ideal marriage that society promotes is often an illusion. True love and commitment are not about meeting expectations but about building meaningful, authentic relationships. By redefining marriage on our own terms, we can create relationships that are rooted in self-awareness, emotional connection, and true partnership.

"Don't let overthinking lead you to judge situations or people too quickly, especially when trust is still in its early stages. When you carry negative predispositions from past experiences, you may unknowingly project them onto new people or situations, seeing problems where there are none. This kind of mindset not only clouds your judgment but can also create distance before connection even begins. Often, what seems grim at first glance is just unfamiliar, not untrustworthy. Approach new bonds with cautious optimism. Give space for clarity to emerge. Positivity doesn't mean being blind, it means being open enough to let the truth reveal itself before deciding what it means."

Chapter 11

STORIES OF SILENCE AND FADING IN DARKNESS

Storyline 6: A bond lost in the air

Vaibhav had been exploring matrimony apps for quite some time. He wasn't desperate, but he was hopeful scrolling through profiles had become a part of his routine, almost like checking news or email. His expectations were modest: a good-looking girl with a pleasant personality, someone with whom life could feel light.

One evening, he came across Aneri's profile. Her pictures caught his eye instantly—not just for her looks, but her calm demeanour, her interests in books and travel, and the way she described herself. Something about her felt balanced. He sent a request, hoping she'd notice him in the crowd.

To his surprise, Aneri accepted.

They began talking on the app. The conversations were casual, polite, and flowed with surprising ease for the first few days. Vaibhav was quick to express interest. Aneri, however, maintained a neutral tone. Then, just as suddenly, she disappeared—no messages, no updates.

Restless and curious, Vaibhav searched for her on Facebook and sent her a message. Days passed without a reply. Then, one day, he received a simple emoji from her—a half-smiling face. It was nothing, and yet to Vaibhav, it was everything. He lit up.

He replied instantly, and from there, a slow, uneven friendship took shape.

They began speaking on and off. Sometimes, they'd exchange voice notes. Sometimes, silence stretched for weeks. Vaibhav kept trying. He was drawn to her—not just for how she looked, but because she felt like an anchor he was silently seeking.

But Aneri had been clear from early on.

"There's no possibility of marriage, Vaibhav. We're from different castes. My family would never agree," she had messaged once.

"That's okay. Let's just talk," he had replied, brushing away the warning with hope.

Aneri was simultaneously speaking to someone else on the same matrimony platform. He was well-settled, good earner, and came from a family that fit her expectations. Aneri didn't hide it either. She had told Vaibhav about it, albeit vaguely.

Vaibhav, on the other hand, was still finding his footing in life. He was smart, observant, and emotionally intuitive—but not yet successful by societal standards. He was still figuring out his path, still making peace with professional instability and personal uncertainty.

Aneri, though raised in a modest middle-class family, had always dreamed of financial stability. For her, marriage wasn't just about love or connection—it was about future security, about ticking boxes that she had been taught to value.

Yet Vaibhav kept hoping. He kept asking her to meet. "Maybe someday," she'd say, often dodging gently.

Vaibhav and Aneri finally met. Their first meeting was quiet, warm, and filled with the comfort of familiarity built over months of virtual exchange. Something shifted after that. The conversations deepened. Aneri began sharing more—her thoughts, her routines, even her insecurities.

One evening, while sipping chai near the lake, she told Vaibhav, "The guy I was talking to... he's from IIT. Earns incredibly well. It was all going fine, but somewhere, it started falling apart. I'm not the career-focused kind he expected. I design from home. It's small scale. He didn't get that."

Vaibhav listened quietly. Hope bloomed again.

They grew closer. Calls became longer. Vaibhav expressed his feelings often—sometimes gently, sometimes with desperation. He felt a sense of belonging around her, but also an undercurrent of insecurity he couldn't shake.

Aneri, beautiful and self-aware, had her circle. Among them was Paresh—her best friend. A married man. Financially stable. Charismatic. Deeply involved in her life.

Vaibhav always found something unsettling about Paresh. It wasn't just that he brought gifts to Aneri and her parents. It was the quiet authority he seemed to hold over her. The way Aneri spoke about him with reverence. The way her parents, though progressive, never questioned his dominant presence.

More disturbing was what Vaibhav gradually learned that Paresh had access to her phone location. He often tracked where she was. Aneri never told Paresh about Vaibhav. She kept a separate phone to speak to him.

"Why hide?" Vaibhav asked once.

Aneri looked down. "Because it's complicated. Paresh is just... part of my life. You wouldn't understand."

He did understand. More than she thought.

Vaibhav started visiting her house. Her family welcomed him. But even there, he could feel it—that invisible thread Paresh had woven around the household. He wasn't just a friend. He was a presence that lingered in their choices, in Aneri's restraint, in the silences she never explained.

Vaibhav didn't know if it was love or obsession anymore. All he knew was, he had fallen for a girl who spoke with kindness, carried her contradictions softly, and lived a life tethered between emotional loyalty and quiet rebellion.

Their bond kept growing. Aneri had started opening up more than ever. She began sharing things with Vaibhav that she hadn't shared with anyone else. There was a comfort, a rhythm to their interactions. Vaibhav, now emotionally anchored, was ready to marry her. Aneri too had started contemplating the idea—testing the feeling of being with him, long-term.

On Vaibhav's birthday, he decided to confront a thought that had been bothering him. The celebration was light, the air filled with close friends and laughter. But Vaibhav couldn't ignore the weight in his heart.

That night, he asked Aneri, "What if Paresh still interferes after we're engaged? After we're married?"

Aneri looked at him with concern. "He won't. I'll make sure of it."

Vaibhav shook his head slightly. "But he tracks your location. He influences your life decisions. You talk about him like he owns a part of you. If your parents are okay with your freedom, then who is he to question or control it?"

Aneri didn't answer immediately. She understood the question. But her silence said more than words could.

Vaibhav, ever rational, couldn't comprehend why a grown, independent woman would allow such intrusion and still call it friendship. He wasn't asking her to abandon anyone—only to **reclaim her boundaries**. But love doesn't always evolve with logic. And that night, the gap between them didn't close.

From that day, the gap between them kept growing. Vaibhav had started a new job with a financial institution and was finally finding his professional rhythm. Aneri was genuinely happy for him. To her, this meant he was now more suitable, more desirable. But to Vaibhav, something began to shift.

The more he evolved, the less aligned Aneri seemed. Her unwillingness to confront Paresh or set boundaries began to appear not just as emotional dependence—but as something that contradicted Vaibhav's sense of freedom and logic.

He started talking to her less. His focus shifted. The same charm that once longed for Aneri now started attracting others. At his new workplace, he noticed admiration from women he never thought would look twice at him. And he realized—he didn't have to keep begging for love.

Eventually, Vaibhav made a decision. If Aneri couldn't draw a line with Paresh, he wouldn't force a future that always felt half-approved.

As Vaibhav distanced himself, Aneri grew restless. She confronted him—not in anger, but in frustration. "Why don't you call me unless I ask you to?"

He didn't answer directly. Because by now, the silence had taken root.

Gradually, the conversations faded. The calls stopped. Vaibhav immersed himself in work. His mind was occupied, and so was his heart—beginning to notice someone else in his office who looked at him without complications.

Aneri felt the void, but she didn't chase him. She tried to bring things back to normal a few times, but it was too late. Vaibhav had moved on—not with resentment, but with quiet acceptance.

Reflection: A Love Lost in the Dark

Sometimes love doesn't die—it simply fades where clarity doesn't exist. Vaibhav was right in questioning control and dominance. But he didn't communicate his withdrawal clearly. Aneri, too, started loving him, but never prioritized the boundaries that could have saved their relationship. Her parents didn't interfere, thinking everything was normal, while the emotional gap widened silently.

The lesson here is clear: be honest about what you want, protect what you value, and never delay confronting what feels off. Love may be patient, but closure is not always guaranteed.

Some stories don't end in fights—they end in unread messages, missed calls, and the kind of silence that says everything.

Storyline 7: When Fire Met Stillness

The sangeet was loud, colourful, and alive with music. Alok stood near the edge of the courtyard, sipping quietly on a glass of soda, observing the dance floor like an outsider at his own gathering. The bride was his cousin, and the guest list was long. Everyone around him seemed to know how to celebrate. He, as always, preferred stillness.

That's when he noticed her.

Surabhi twirled barefoot on the dance floor. Her silver anklets chimed louder than the DJ, and her smile held no hesitation. She wasn't trying to impress anyone—she was simply being. And for the first time in years, Alok couldn't look away.

Their first conversation was as spontaneous as the rain that evening. She was looking for the dessert counter. He pointed silently, and she smiled wide enough to thank him without words.

"You don't talk much, do you?" she asked playfully.

Alok smirked. "I talk when I have something real to say."

"Ah," she nodded, mock-serious. "A man of few words and deep thoughts. Dangerous." They laughed. And something shifted.

What started as casual small talk became midnight walks, shared playlists, long text chains, and eventually, unspoken rituals—he'd wait for her call after her rehearsals; she'd text him random thoughts at odd hours. Slowly, Alok found himself looking forward to moments he once thought were unnecessary distractions.

But what Surabhi didn't know was that Alok was also in conversation with a few others—emotionally unavailable, unsure, and unsure of what he really wanted. He was not dishonest, but he was distracted. Between work, social obligations, and his own internal chaos, he couldn't give her the full attention she deserved. And deep down, he knew it.

She didn't ask him to change. But something inside him began to.

Three months in, the differences started showing. Surabhi wanted to talk—about feelings, fears, future plans. Alok somehow couldn't open up. He was processing, slowly, cautiously.

"You don't let me in," Surabhi said one evening. "You talk, but only to a line. Then you shut the door."

Alok looked down. "I just don't think everything needs to be said out loud."

She sighed. "But I need to feel seen, Alok. Heard. Not just tolerated."

He said nothing. And that silence, for the first time, felt like distance.

It was a Sunday evening. Surabhi had just returned from a performance that had drained her. She called him. He answered but sounded distracted.

"Can we meet?" she asked. "I feel low."

A pause. He said, "Today is really packed. Maybe tomorrow?"

The call ended quietly. So did something else. That night, Surabhi texted:

"I've loved you without reservation. But I can't keep showing up alone. When you're ready to stop hiding from love, maybe you'll remember what this could've been."

She didn't block him. She didn't lash out. She just stopped.

Few months passed. Alok didn't respond. He read her message again and again. He didn't know how to fight back and apologize.

He tried dating with other girls again—briefly, blandly.

No one laughed like Surabhi. No one challenged his silences with light. No one tried hard to know him. No one even tried to talk deeply.

One year later. Alok was invited to speak at a panel on creative finance for artists. As he adjusted the mic, he caught a familiar voice echo from backstage.

Surabhi.

She was hosting the evening, now working with an arts NGO. Her voice was confident, her energy intact. She looked at him once during the introduction—and smiled. Warm, distant, polite.

After the event, they met for coffee. Talked. Laughed. There was no bitterness.

"You look peaceful and gorgeous," he said.

"I am," she replied. "I learned how to stop loving people who don't know how to love themselves."

Alok swallowed the lump in his throat. She laughed hard. He wanted to say something. Anything. But he couldn't.

She had moved on and found someone.

They never met again. Not because of anger, but because some stories aren't meant to be rewritten—they're meant to be remembered.

Alok never forgot her. He carried her laugh, her lightness, her wild honesty. She became his forever regret.

Because not every love ends in a relationship. Some end in realisation.

Reflection: Why Alok Stayed Silent

Alok's silence wasn't born out of apathy—it came from emotional conditioning, fear, and internal conflict. He was never taught how to handle vulnerability. He was also preoccupied—with his career, social conversations, and unresolved emotional clutter. When Surabhi left, he felt the loss deeply but became paralyzed by guilt and self-doubt. Like many emotionally reserved individuals, he assumed that saying nothing was safer than saying the wrong thing. What he didn't realize is that in love, silence can speak louder than any mistake.

By the time Alok began to understand the depth of what he had lost, Surabhi had already chosen to protect her peace and move on. This is the quiet truth behind many modern relationships: not all fail because of a lack of love—some fade because of a lack of presence. And by the time one is ready to speak, the moment may have already passed.

"Love cannot be demanded; it can only be inspired. You don't get love by asking for it, chasing it, or begging for attention. The only way to receive love is to be lovable, through kindness, care, presence, and sincerity. Love grows in the soil of generosity. When you give love freely, without keeping score or attaching expectations, something magical happens, it often comes back to you, not equally, but in beautiful, compounded ways."

Chapter 12

READINESS VS. PRESSURE: PREPARING YOURSELF FOR MARRIAGE

Marriage is often seen as a natural milestone in life, but true readiness for marriage goes beyond age, societal timelines, or family expectations. It requires a deep understanding of oneself, emotional maturity, and clarity about personal desires and goals. This chapter explores how individuals can assess their readiness for marriage, differentiate between internal desire and external pressure, and approach this life decision with self-awareness, rationality, and emotional balance.

Understanding What It Means to Be Ready for Marriage

Marriage readiness transcends the typical metrics of age or financial stability—it delves deep into emotional and mental preparedness. It's about the willingness to invest time, energy, and emotions into constructing a life with another person. This involves the capacity to handle conflicts, disagreements, and the myriad daily challenges that accompany marriage. Are you prepared to share responsibilities, make compromises, and grow alongside your partner?

Several key indicators can help determine if one is truly ready for marriage:

- **Emotional Maturity**: Recognizing that love is not perpetually blissful and requires continuous effort and adaptation.

- **Self-awareness**: Having a clear understanding of one's needs, desires, and non-negotiables in a relationship is crucial. It's about knowing what you can tolerate, what you need from a partnership, and what you can offer.

- **Independence**: This involves the ability to feel content and complete on your own, without the need for someone else to "complete" you. True readiness for marriage means you're not seeking a partner out of need but rather out of a desire to share your already fulfilling life.

Being ready for marriage means more than just wanting to get married; it's about being prepared to face the intricacies of a shared life and having the tools to build a sustainable and rewarding relationship.

Differentiating Between Internal Desire and External Pressure

The decision to marry is often tangled between genuine personal desire and the weight of external expectations. Many individuals encounter significant pressure from family expectations, cultural norms, or societal timelines, which can cloud their true desires. Common refrains like "All my friends are getting married—I guess I should too," or "My family keeps reminding me I'm getting older," exemplify how societal cues can urge one towards marriage, irrespective of personal readiness or intent.

The core issue here is the influence of external pressures:

- External pressures can precipitate rushed decisions that may not genuinely align with an individual's values or desires for life. The fear of falling behind peers or satisfying familial expectations can overshadow personal readiness.

- There's a tendency to select partners based on societal checklists—attributes deemed "appropriate" or "desirable" by societal standards—rather than on the basis of true compatibility and personal connection.

To navigate this complex interplay of internal desires versus external expectations, reflecting on certain critical questions can be enlightening:

- "Do I want to get married because I truly feel ready, or because others expect it of me?" This question helps in identifying if the motivation to marry is autonomous or influenced by external factors.

- "Am I seeking a partner to complement my life or to fill a void?" This helps determine whether the pursuit of marriage is for the right reasons—enhancement of life through partnership, rather than a remedy for loneliness or incompleteness.

- "Would I still want to get married if there was no societal pressure?" Removing the external factor from the equation can provide clearer insight into one's genuine desires.

Understanding the distinction between internal desire and external pressure is crucial. It enables individuals to make more authentic decisions that are likely to lead to long-term satisfaction and partnership success.

The Importance of Self-Love and Emotional Independence

A healthy relationship with oneself is the foundation of any robust partnership. You cannot expect to build a healthy, sustainable relationship with another if you have not cultivated one with yourself. Self-love is essential—it fosters stronger emotional resilience, which is crucial during conflicts within a relationship. It nurtures a sense of self-worth that remains independent of your partner, and it empowers you to set and respect healthy boundaries.

The absence of self-love can lead to several relational pitfalls:

- **Seeking Validation**: Without a solid foundation of self-love, individuals may constantly seek validation from their partner, which can lead to an unbalanced relationship where one's self-esteem is heavily dependent on another's reassurance and approval.

- **Loss of Identity**: There's a significant risk of losing one's identity in the relationship. When one does not value themselves enough independently, they might continuously Mold their likes, dislikes, and even their personality to fit into the perceived expectations of their partner.

- **Dependency and Power Struggles**: Dependency, stemming from a lack of emotional independence, can create significant emotional imbalances and power struggles within a relationship. This can lead to conflicts where one partner may feel burdened or the other might feel undervalued.

The adage that "marriage should be a union of two whole individuals, not two halves seeking completion" encapsulates the importance of entering into a marriage as a complete individual. This does not mean you must be perfect, but rather that you are aware of your intrinsic value and do not look to a partner to define or complete you. This perspective ensures that both partners can contribute to the relationship from a place of strength and personal completeness, fostering a healthier, more balanced union.

Evaluating Your Emotional Readiness

Emotional readiness is a crucial yet often overlooked aspect of preparing for marriage. It encompasses the ability to manage one's emotions healthily and constructively within the context of a close relationship. Assessing emotional readiness involves introspection and honesty about one's ability to engage in deep emotional exchanges and conflict resolution.

Questions to assess emotional readiness include:

- **Open Communication**: "Can I communicate openly about my feelings and needs?" This question examines whether you can express yourself clearly and openly, a vital component of healthy relationships.

- **Conflict Resolution**: "Am I able to handle conflicts without emotional shutdown or aggression?" This probes your strategies for dealing with disagreements, a common aspect of any relationship, and whether you can remain constructive under stress.

- **Emotional Support**: "Do I have the capacity to support my partner emotionally, even during difficult times?" This assesses your ability to be a source of strength and support, which is essential during the inevitable challenges that life presents.

Signs you may not be emotionally ready for marriage:

- **Carrying Past Emotional Baggage**: If you still carry unresolved feelings or trauma from past relationships, it might cloud your emotional availability and impact your interactions with a future spouse.

- **Struggling with Vulnerability**: Difficulty in being vulnerable or expressing emotions can hinder the development of intimacy and trust in a relationship. If you find it hard to let your guard down and share your innermost thoughts, it may be a sign to work on these areas before committing to marriage.

- **Avoidance of Difficult Conversations**: If you tend to avoid challenging conversations or fear conflict, it might indicate an unreadiness to face the complex dynamics that marriage involves. Effective communication and the ability to tackle tough issues head-on are pivotal for a successful marriage.

Understanding and improving these aspects of emotional readiness can not only prepare you better for marriage but also enhance your personal growth and emotional health.

Building a Personal Framework for Choosing a Partner

In the quest for a lifelong partner, it's beneficial to adopt a strategic approach, much like Warren Buffett's investment philosophy of "only swinging at balls within your circle of competence." This means recognizing which opportunities—or in this case, potential partners—are worth considering based on a clear set of criteria. Just as you don't need to say yes to every investment, you don't need to say yes to every relationship opportunity—only the right ones.

Creating a personal framework involves several layers:

- **Must-Have Traits**: These are non-negotiable characteristics that form the foundation of a successful relationship. They might include core values such as integrity, emotional intelligence for understanding and managing emotions, respect for each other, and alignment in life goals. These traits ensure that the basic, most critical aspects of a partner align with your expectations and needs.

- **Should-Have Traits**: These are preferable traits but are more flexible compared to must-haves. They can include hobbies, lifestyle choices, and other personal preferences that enhance compatibility but are not deal breakers. For

144

instance, sharing a common interest in travel or books might be desirable but not essential.

- **Deal-Breakers**: These are absolute no-go that you cannot compromise on. Common deal-breakers include issues like disrespect, dishonesty, or any other behaviour or value that you find unacceptable. Identifying these helps to immediately rule out potential partners who exhibit these traits.

This framework is inherently flexible and can adapt as you grow and evolve. "As you grow, your list evolves—but having a basic structure helps filter out incompatible partners early on." By having a clear, structured approach to evaluating potential partners, you can navigate the complex dating landscape more effectively, ensuring that you engage more deeply with those who truly align with your values and life vision. This method not only streamlines the process of finding a compatible partner but also enhances the quality of your romantic engagements, leading to more fulfilling relationships.

Overcoming Fear of Commitment and Overthinking

Fear of commitment is a common barrier to entering into long-term relationships and can stem from past traumas, fear of failure, or the habit of overthinking potential risks. This fear can manifest in several ways:

- Fear of Making the Wrong Choice: The worry that one might choose the wrong partner can lead to significant anxiety, preventing commitment.

- Over-analysis Analysing every possible detail about the relationship or potential partner can lead to decision paralysis, where no decision feels right.

- Doubt in Handling Responsibilities: Doubting one's ability to handle the responsibilities of marriage can also deter commitment.

Solutions to Overcome Fears

- Acknowledging Fears: Recognize and understand your fears but don't let them control your decisions. Accepting that fear is a natural part of the decision-making process can help you approach it more rationally.

- Focusing on Progress, Not Perfection: Understanding that no partner will tick every box or be perfect can alleviate some of the pressures of making the "perfect" choice.

- Practicing Emotional Resilience: Building resilience helps you understand that while challenges will arise, you have the skills and resources to navigate them effectively.

The Role of Rationality and Emotional Intuition

Decisions about marriage require a delicate balance between rational thought and emotional intuition. Here's why both are essential:

- Emotions: While emotions are crucial, relying solely on them can lead to decisions based on temporary feelings like infatuation.

- Rationality: Conversely, solely relying on logic might lead to overlooking the emotional depth and connection that make relationships fulfilling.

Finding balance involves:

- Rational Frameworks: Use rational criteria such as compatibility, shared values, and long-term goals to evaluate potential partners systematically.

- Trusting Emotional Intuition: Allow your emotional instincts to guide you towards sensing deeper connections and compatibility that go beyond logical analysis.

Handling Societal Comparisons and External Expectations

It's natural to compare your relationship progress to others, especially when societal norms and timelines pressure you. These comparisons can create undue pressure and self-doubt, leading to rushed decisions just to "keep up."

To counteract these pressures:

- Personal Focus: Concentrate on your own journey and timeline, rather than conforming to societal expectations.

- Reality of Social Media: Remind yourself that social media often represents a curated, highlight reel of others' lives and not the complete picture.

- Celebrate Personal Growth: Value your self-awareness, personal development, and readiness for a relationship more than external milestones.

Understanding the Long-Term Commitment of Marriage

Marriage extends beyond the realms of romance into continuous partnership, compromise, and mutual growth:

- Challenges of Marriage: Be prepared for emotional fluctuations, conflicts, and significant life changes that test adaptability.

- Keys to Lasting Marriage: Foster respect, emotional intimacy, shared life goals, and the ability to grow both individually and together.

Love Marriage vs. Arranged Marriage: What Should I Choose?

I've been torn between two worlds. One that says, *"Trust love, find your person,"* and another that says, *"Let your family help—it's safer, faster, and more rooted."* Honestly, both paths have their risks. Love marriages offer freedom, but not always certainty. Arranged marriages offer structure, but not always depth.

I've seen people fall deeply in love and still fall apart. I've seen strangers become soulmates after a well-matched arrangement. So, which one is right? I don't think it's about love vs. arranged anymore. It's about how aware I am when making the choice. Do I know myself well enough to choose someone without emotional illusions? Can I speak my truth if I'm going through an arranged setup, rather than pretend to agree under pressure?

What matters to me now is alignment—emotional, mental, and practical. Whether I find it on my own or through my family, I'll call it love either way. Because the real question isn't *"How did you meet?"*—it's *"Did you choose each other fully after you met?"*

What Is the Right Age to Get Married?

I used to believe there was a perfect age. Society certainly made it seem that way—25, 28, or maximum by 30. Beyond that, I was warned: "Good matches vanish, responsibilities increase, and people start judging." And for a while, I internalized all of that. I felt like I was running out of time, even when I wasn't ready emotionally.

But the truth is, age doesn't guarantee readiness. I've met people in their 20s who treat marriage like a task list and people in their 30s still unsure of what commitment means.

For me, the right age to marry is when I know who I am, what I want, and how I handle both love and loneliness. It's not when society says the time is right—but when I feel internally calm about the idea of building a life with someone.

I may still feel pressure sometimes. I may still compare timelines. But deep down, I know that the cost of marrying unprepared is far higher than the cost of marrying late.

Knowing When to Wait and When to Take the Leap

While timing in relationships is crucial, waiting for a perfect moment to commit can be futile:

- Assessing Reasons to Wait: Question whether your hesitation is based on fear or valid reasons. Reflect on your current emotional, mental, and financial readiness.

- Valid Reasons to Wait: It's reasonable to delay commitment if you're focusing on personal growth, healing from past wounds, or need more time to understand your desires.

- Right Time to Leap: Consider taking the step if you've found someone who matches your core values, and you feel prepared for the challenges and growth that come with a shared life.

Approaching marriage with a well-rounded perspective, equipped with self-awareness, rational assessment, and emotional intuition, can lead to more meaningful and enduring partnerships. By internalizing these insights, individuals can navigate the complexities of relationships with greater confidence and clarity, ultimately making choices that align with their deepest values and life goals.

"

In most early-stage relationships or even casual acquaintance, the burden of initiative often falls on men to start conversations, express feelings, propose commitment, or set the direction of where things might go. Many women, knowingly or unknowingly, expect men to take the first step. This has created a cycle where men are positioned as the chasers, while women observe, evaluate, and decide based on effort, consistency, and emotional safety.

But there's a deeper reason behind this hesitance, many women hold back emotionally because their past experiences taught them a hard lesson: expressing too soon can lead to regret. So, they stay guarded. They test reliability. They wait for a pattern to build before opening up.

And ironically, just when they start expressing themselves and get comfortable, men often begin to show their true intent. In many cases, that intent is far from emotional depth. Some men who stayed patient only to fulfil a physical agenda suddenly shift behaviour, leaving the woman confused, disappointed, and disillusioned.

That's why more women today have started asking blunt questions early on: *"What are your intentions? What are you looking for?"*

But deep down, do they truly believe men will answer that honestly? Most don't. And that's the tragedy. Because distrust has become a default, not because women want it that way but because experience has made it necessary.

"

Chapter 13

CHOOSING MARRIAGE OR EMBRACING SINGLEHOOD: A PERSONAL CHOICE

In a world where marriage is often seen as the ultimate life milestone, choosing to stay single or delaying marriage is sometimes viewed with scepticism or even pity. However, the idea that happiness and fulfilment only come through marriage is a societal myth that needs re-evaluation. This chapter explores how marriage should be a conscious personal choice, not a societal obligation, and why embracing singlehood can be equally fulfilling and empowering.

In many cultures, particularly in India, marriage is often viewed as a mandatory milestone, deeply ingrained in the societal framework. The pressure to marry can be intense, fuelled by pervasive societal beliefs.

Common Societal Beliefs:

- **Universal Necessity for a Partner**: The belief that everyone needs a life partner to lead a fulfilled life is widespread, reinforcing the idea that singlehood equates to incompleteness.
- **Marriage as a Key to Happiness**: Many hold the conviction that marriage is essential for happiness and

stability, viewing it as the ultimate goal for personal and social stability.

- **Stigma Around Age**: There is a significant stigma attached to remaining unmarried by a certain age, with prevalent thoughts like, "If you're not married by a certain age, something must be wrong," which can create immense pressure to conform.

Impact of These Beliefs:

- **Rushing into Marriage**: Driven by these societal pressures, individuals may rush into marriages without genuine desire or readiness, leading to mismatches and marital dissatisfaction.
- **Stigma Surrounding Singlehood**: Those who delay marriage or choose to remain single often face judgment, pity, or unsolicited advice, suggesting that their life choices are somehow less valid or complete.

Redefining the Purpose of Marriage

Marriage should not be seen as a life requirement but as a personal choice.

Ask yourself:

"Do I want marriage for companionship, growth, and shared life experiences?"

"Or do I want marriage to fit into societal norms or avoid loneliness?"

Healthy reasons to marry:

Emotional connection, shared values, and a desire to build a life together.

Unhealthy reasons to marry:

Fear of loneliness, societal pressure, or the desire to meet family expectations.

Staying Single: A Valid Choice in Various Situations

Choosing to stay single can be a well-considered and appropriate decision under several circumstances. Recognizing when singlehood serves one's best interests is crucial in a society that often prioritizes marriage as the norm. Situations were Staying Single Might Be Right:

- **Personal Discovery**: If you are still in the process of figuring out your own goals, values, or desires, jumping into a partnership can complicate your journey. It's essential to have a solid understanding of oneself to ensure any future relationship is based on genuine compatibility and mutual respect.
- **Emotional Availability**: Following a breakup or any significant emotional trauma, it's crucial to allow time for healing. Rushing into another relationship without fully recovering can lead to further emotional distress and hinder personal growth.
- **Personal Values**: For some individuals, marriage does not align with their life plans. Whether due to philosophical reasons, lifestyle choices, or career commitments, recognizing that marriage is not a compulsory milestone is vital. Respecting this personal choice is key to living authentically.
- **Valuing Independence**: Many people find great fulfilment in their independence, valuing the freedom to control their own time, space, and life choices without compromise. For such individuals, the benefits of singlehood might outweigh those of a committed partnership.

Does Staying Single Always Lead to Loneliness?

Contrary to common misconceptions, singlehood does not inherently lead to loneliness. Loneliness is more accurately described as a lack of meaningful connections, rather than simply the absence of a romantic relationship.

Emotional Fulfilment Outside of Romance: Many single individuals cultivate strong networks of friendships, family bonds, and community ties that provide significant emotional fulfilment and support. These relationships can be deeply satisfying and offer a sense of belonging those combats feelings of loneliness.

Benefits of Being Single

Embracing singlehood offers numerous benefits, including significant personal growth and independence. Being single allows for making life decisions without compromise, providing a unique opportunity for self-discovery. Being single provides the freedom to pursue one's passions, travel, and make life decisions based on personal preferences and without needing to compromise for a partner.

Financial autonomy is another perk, as single individuals control their finances entirely, making decisions that best suit their personal financial goals. Emotionally, singlehood is a time to develop resilience and self-sufficiency, qualities that not only stand one in good stead alone but also enhance any future relationships.

Without the commitments that come with a partnership, single individuals often find more time to invest in and deepen relationships with friends and family, as well as to cultivate a stronger relationship with themselves.

Overall, while societal norms often emphasize the benefits of partnerships, singlehood presents unique opportunities for development and satisfaction, underscoring that being single can be both fulfilling and enriching.

Singlehood offers invaluable time for self-exploration and personal growth, allowing individuals to understand their desires, ambitions, and values without the influence of a partner.

The Fear of Being Single and Its Impact on Decision-Making

The fear of being single—driven by worries about loneliness or societal judgment—can push individuals into rushing into unsuitable or unfulfilling marriages. Consequences of Fear-Driven Decisions:

- **Relationships Based on Need**: Decisions made from fear tend to lead to relationships that are based more on the need to avoid loneliness than on genuine desire or compatibility.
- **Long-Term Dissatisfaction**: Settling out of fear can result in emotional dissatisfaction and regrets, as the relationship may not fulfil deeper needs or desires.

Viewing singlehood not as a mere waiting period before marriage but as a valuable phase for personal growth and discovery can significantly alter one's perspective. This healthier viewpoint encourages embracing singlehood as an opportunity to build a fuller, more self-directed life.

How to Know If You're Ready for Marriage or Singlehood

Deciding between marriage and singlehood involves deep self-reflection. Asking yourself questions like,

"Do I feel fulfilled and happy on my own?", "Am I seeking marriage out of desire or pressure?", or "Can I imagine a future where I'm single and still feel content?" can clarify your readiness.

If you feel emotionally whole and ready to share your life, understand the responsibilities of marriage, and have found a partner who aligns with your core values, you may be ready for marriage. Conversely, if you value your independence, are focused on personal goals, or feel fulfilled alone, singlehood might be suitable for you.

How to Handle Societal Pressure as a Single Person

Handling societal pressure as a single person requires resilience and confidence in your life choices. When faced with questions like, "You're not married yet? Why not?" or "Don't you want someone to take care of you?" setting clear boundaries and shutting down invasive questions politely but firmly can be effective. Surrounding yourself with like-minded individuals who respect your choices, focusing on the positives of singlehood, and practicing self-validation can help you manage societal expectations and maintain your peace.

Choosing Marriage Later in Life

Choosing to marry later in life can offer numerous benefits such as greater emotional maturity, clarity about what you want in a partner, and reduced societal pressure to conform to traditional timelines. The key is to marry when you feel ready, not according to societal expectations.

Redefining Fulfilment—With or Without Marriage

Fulfilment is derived from how authentically you live your life, not whether you are married or single. Both paths can offer profound satisfaction if they align with your personal values and desires. The most crucial relationship is the one you have with yourself; deep self-love and respect can ensure happiness regardless of the path you choose.

- Marriage should be a personal choice, not a response to societal pressure.

- Singlehood can be just as fulfilling as marriage when embraced intentionally.
- Decisions driven by fear of loneliness often lead to unsatisfactory marriages. True commitment should stem from desire, not fear.
- Fulfilment and happiness originate from within, irrespective of marital status.
- There is no universal right time for marriage—each person's journey is unique and should reflect their values and readiness.

"Failure is an event, not your identity. Whether it's a breakup, a divorce, a failed business venture, or a career setback, it's important to remember *something didn't work out, but that doesn't mean you are broken.* The most common mistake people make is internalizing the outcome thinking *"I failed"* instead of *"That experience failed."* This emotional misstep can erode self-worth, trap you in guilt, and create walls that block future growth. But real healing begins with self-love—the kind that doesn't depend on anyone's validation. From the moment you become an adult until your last breath, the most important relationship you'll ever have is with yourself. Self-love is not arrogance, it's the quiet confidence that says, *"I am enough, even when life falls apart."* When self-love becomes your foundation, resilience becomes your superpower. You don't pretend everything is okay, you acknowledge the pain, learn the lesson, and get back up. Moving on is not betrayal to the past; it is a promise to your future. Stay authentic. Stay you. Because the world may shake your foundations, but your essence, your quirks, dreams, and truth must remain untouched. You are not your failures. You are the strength that rises from them."

CONCLUSION

Storyline 1 Continued....

After months of tension and half-hearted compromises, Ashish finally sat down with his parents. He had to speak. Aarti had given him a clear ultimatum: she would not return unless the daily emotional strain ended.

When he shared this with his parents, they were shocked.

"We don't need such girls in this house," his mother said, her voice trembling with disbelief. "Girls who want to separate us from our only son?"

His father stayed silent, but the hurt was visible on his face.

Ashish stood still for a moment, but something in him cracked open. Years of silence, emotional suppression, and people-pleasing had taken a toll.

And for the first time, he said what he had been holding inside:

"I wasn't ready for marriage. It was *you*, Mom, who insisted. You said if I got married, everything would become better at home. But did it? Or have we made things even more difficult for ourselves?

Now, you both constantly interfere in our lives. Aarti and I are struggling to even breathe. And it's not because we don't care— it's because we're trying to balance two worlds that keep clashing."

He continued, his voice now firm, clear, and grounded:

"I care for Aarti. And I respect you both just as much. But I want to live a life with her—peacefully. So, either she stays here, and you stop interfering... don't expect household work from her or judge her every move.

Or Aarti and I stay separately. But I won't let this spiral further."

His parents were stunned. They had never seen Ashish like this—so certain, so assertive. Deep down, they knew how much he meant to them. And they couldn't bear the thought of drifting apart.

Ashish added, "Let's not compare our house with others. Times have changed. People don't get married just so someone can help with chores. They get married to share life, meaningfully. And if it's about the household—I can cook, clean, do whatever is needed. Let's move past these old expectations."

Silence lingered.

Then, something shifted in his mother. Maybe it was the pain in Ashish's eyes. Maybe it was her own guilt. But she picked up the phone and called Aarti. Her voice, now soft and sincere, carried something it never had before—*accountability*.

She apologized. Genuinely. She asked her to come back. To try again—not just as a daughter-in-law, but as a person, a part of the family, with her own identity and choices.

Later that evening, I was with Ashish when Aarti called.

We spoke on video for two hours—listening, healing, even laughing by the end. The conversation wasn't perfect, but it was honest. That was enough.

Aarti came back two days later.

Ashish was the happiest I had seen him in months.

Two weeks passed, and Ashish invited me for dinner at his home. When I entered, both he and Aarti welcomed me with warm smiles. Over dinner, they thanked me for simply being there. For listening. For nudging. For holding space when everything felt like it was falling apart.

We sat for hours that night—talking about life, about change, about marriage and growing up.

Ashish had someone to turn to in his moment of confusion.

But that evening, a question lingered in my mind:

What about all the other Ashish out there? The ones who don't have a friend to help them see clearly. The ones who feel stuck, unheard, and lost between love and loyalty?

Where do they go when their hearts are in conflict and their homes feel like battlegrounds?

Who helps them break the silence, soften the ego, and rebuild love with dignity?

Navigating Love, Marriage, and the Journey of Self-Discovery: Finding Clarity Amidst the Paradox

As we reach the end of this exploration into love, marriage, and personal fulfilment, one undeniable truth emerges—there is no universal path to happiness. Society has long positioned marriage as the ultimate milestone, an inevitable step in life's journey. However, in reality, love and commitment are deeply personal choices, and their success is not measured by societal validation but by personal fulfilment, emotional growth, and mutual respect.

Growth comes not from avoiding pain but from understanding it, processing it, and moving forward with newfound wisdom.

Success in love is not about longevity or societal approval; it is about finding depth, connection, and authenticity. A short-lived relationship filled with mutual respect and genuine moments can be more fulfilling than a lifetime spent in an emotionally disconnected marriage. Love, whether shared with a partner or cultivated within oneself, should be about fulfilment, growth, and the freedom to be your true self.

At its core, the paradox of love and marriage is that there are no absolute answers—only the questions we ask ourselves and the choices we make along the way. The key is to approach life, love, and relationships with self-awareness, honesty, and the courage to follow your heart, whether that leads to marriage, singlehood, or something entirely unique. Ultimately, happiness is not about conforming to a script written by society but about creating a life that aligns with your values, desires, and vision for fulfilment.

Life is uncertain, and no one can predict what lies ahead. Love, marriage, relationships—each path is filled with unknowns, twists, and surprises. The future is not in our control, but what we can control is how we approach it.

We may not know where life will take us, but we can consciously shape it by making thoughtful choices, staying true to ourselves, and embracing change with an open heart.

Whether we choose to walk the journey alone or with a partner, whether we face love or heartbreak, the beauty of life lies in its unpredictability. And in that uncertainty, there is endless possibility for growth, happiness, and fulfilment—if we dare to step forward with courage and intention.

No matter what path you choose, choose it with intention, self-respect, and hope.

REFERENCES

- Ainsworth, Mary D. Salter, and John Bowlby. "An Ethological Approach to Personality Development." *American Psychologist*, vol. 46, no. 4, 1991, pp. 333–341.
- Bauman, Zygmunt. *Liquid Love: On the Frailty of Human Bonds*. Polity Press, 2003.
- Becker, Gary S. *A Treatise on the Family*. Harvard University Press, 1981.
- Beck, Ulrich, and Elisabeth Beck-Gernsheim. *Individualization: Institutionalized Individualism and its Social and Political Consequences*. SAGE Publications, 2002.
- Festinger, Leon. *A Theory of Cognitive Dissonance*. Stanford University Press, 1957.
- Goffman, Erving. *The Presentation of Self in Everyday Life*. Anchor Books, 1959.
- Ipsos. "Global Trends: Marriage and Relationships." *Ipsos*, 2021, www.ipsos.com.
- Kierkegaard, Søren. *The Works of Love*. Translated by Howard V. Hong and Edna H. Hong, Princeton University Press, 1995.
- Maslow, Abraham H. *Motivation and Personality*. Harper & Row, 1954.
- May, Rollo. *Love and Will*. W. W. Norton & Company, 1969.
- McKinsey & Company. "The Future of Women at Work." *McKinsey Global Institute*, 2019, www.mckinsey.com.
- Pew Research Center. "Marriage and Cohabitation in the U.S." *Pew Research Center*, 2020, www.pewresearch.org.
- Sartre, Jean-Paul. *Being and Nothingness*. Translated by Hazel E. Barnes, Washington Square Press, 1956.

ACKNOWLEDGEMENTS

To my friends, cousins, and acquaintances—thank you for opening up, for speaking honestly about your experiences, and for trusting me with your stories. Your perspectives have been instrumental in shaping the emotional and psychological depth of this book.

Each narrative and insight shared with me helped piece together the larger picture of how love and relationships are evolving in today's world. While identities have been changed to respect privacy, the emotions and dilemmas remain true to what so many of us go through.

I owe this book not just to my research and writing—but to all of you who allowed me to listen and learn.

With sincere gratitude,

Darshan

ABOUT AUTHOR

Darshan is an author, observer, and advisor who bridges psychology, philosophy, and social reality through his writing. With an MBA in Finance and a background in investing, his perspective is both analytical and empathetic. He has spent over a decade analysing trends—not only in markets and industries, but in human behaviour and societal evolution.

Over the years, Darshan has written extensively through blogs and articles about the intersection of society, relationships, personal growth, and emotional decision-making. The idea for this book was born out of countless conversations—with friends, family, acquaintances, and strangers—each navigating their own version of the love, relationship, and marriage dilemma.

Through deep listening, personal reflection, and psychological inquiry, he noticed patterns that felt universal. In The Paradox of Modern Love and Relationships, he weaves those observations into stories, reflections, and thought frameworks that empower young people to think for themselves, question inherited assumptions, and make conscious decisions about love and marriage.

This is Darshan's second book, following his well-received debut Future Ready Investing, a strategic guide to investing in India's emerging sectors and demographic trends.

9 7 9 8 8 8 9 9 2 9 5 2 1 8